Hominids
A Look Back
At Our Ancestors

HELEN RONEY SATTLER

Hominids
A LOOK BACK
AT OUR ANCESTORS

ILLUSTRATED BY CHRISTOPHER SANTORO

LOTHROP, LEE & SHEPARD BOOKS   NEW YORK

ACKNOWLEDGMENTS

I am greatly indebted to several individuals for various forms of assistance. I am especially grateful to Dr. James McKenna, chairman, department of anthropology, Pomona College, for reading the completed manuscript and for offering valuable suggestions and information along the way, as well as for checking the drawings for accuracy.

I also extend thanks to Dr. S. L. Washburn and Jane Lancaster for allowing me to discuss this project with them. In addition to those whose work appears in the Bibliography, I am grateful to the following authors for information gleaned from their papers published in scientific journals and books: Noel Boaz, C. L. Brace, Gunter Brauer, Henry Bunn, Garniss H. Curtis, Raymond A. Dart, M. H. Day, Jared Diamond, Dean Falk, David Frayer, John Gribbin, J.B.S. Haldane, Allen L. Hammond, Lancelot Hogben, Glynn Isaac, William L. Jungers, Lawrence H. Keeley, Richard G. Klein, Jeffrey Kurland, Jeffrey T. Laitman, Jane Lancaster, Mary Leakey, C. Owen Lovejoy, Henry M. McHenry, Kevin McKean, Ernst Mayr, E. Orowan, Hal Porter, Douglas Preston, Boyce Rensberger, G. Phillip Rightmore, J. T. Robinson, Romuald Schild, Pat Shipman, Fred H. Smith, Frank Spencer, Lawrence G. Straus, M. Taieb, Phillip V. Tobias, Erik Trinkaus, Tim D. White, Milford H. Wolpoff, R.V.S. Wright, J. Wymer, and others too numerous to mention.

890155

Text copyright © 1988 by Helen Roney Sattler.
Illustrations copyright © 1988 by Christopher Santoro.

Library of Congress Cataloging in Publication Data
Sattler, Helen Roney. Hominids: a look back at our ancestors.
Bibliography: p.117. Summary: Discusses the various hominids which preceded man as we know him today, as deduced from their fossil remains. 1. Fossil man—Juvenile literature. [1. Man, Prehistoric. 2. Fossil man] I. Santoro, Christopher, ill. II. Title. GN282.S28 1988 573.3 86-810624
ISBN 0-688-06061-7

To Dorothy Briley,
without whom this book
would not have existed

H. R. S.

To Carmen

C. S.

CONTENTS

FOREWORD

When, where, and why did our ancestors begin to walk upright, make stone tools, and come to depend upon a large brain? How and when did they migrate out of the warm tropics into colder regions of Europe and Asia? When did early humans discover fire, engage in gathering, participate in opportunistic hunting, and start to bury their dead? When might our species have begun to speak?

Anthropologists do not yet have the complete answers to these questions, but what we do know is beautifully presented in this highly accurate, thorough, and exciting book by Helen Sattler. She captures and communicates something that every anthropologist, archeologist, and paleontologist knows: that the search for human biological and cultural origins, although frustratingly difficult, never stops being truly fascinating and highly rewarding.

Mrs. Sattler takes all of us on a highly successful journey in which the relationship between tools and technology, so important to contemporary human beings, is shown to have had a very close connection with changing environments and the biology of human actors as they adapt to these environments. Sticking close to the meaning of artifacts left behind by earlier human forms, Mrs. Sattler shows us how tools and, hence, culture changed at an extremely slow pace over a million and a half years, but how this slow change began to accelerate faster and faster as certain technological breakthroughs were achieved and human evolution approached more modern periods.

Mrs. Sattler has made a significant contribution in conveying with such clarity the recentness of history and urban life and the truly special characteristics that distinguish our species.

James J. McKenna
Associate Professor of Anthropology
Chair, Department of Sociology and Anthropology
Pomona College
Claremont, California

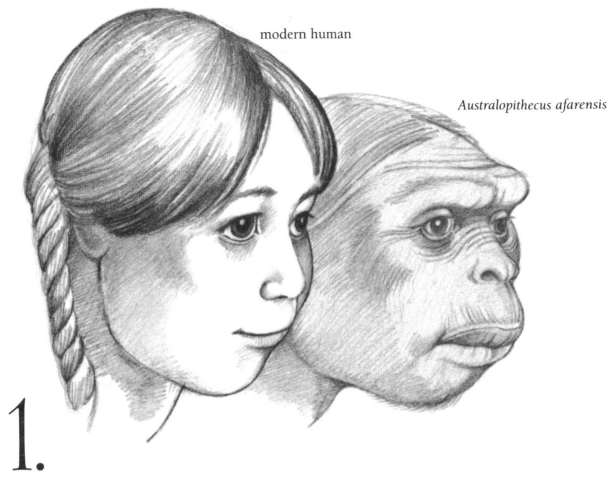

modern human

Australopithecus afarensis

1.
THE HUMAN FAMILY

HUMANS OR HUMANLIKE CREATURES HAVE BEEN ON EARTH FOR at least four and a half million years. We know this because scientists have found their remains. It was once imagined that these creatures were savage killer apemen. The fossil evidence shows that they actually may have been peaceful and cooperative.

The earliest humanlike creatures didn't look exactly like us. For that matter, neither did our own great-great-grandparents. Like all living things, humans change little by little over many generations. There is probably a strong enough resemblance between you and your great-great-grandparents to show that you belong to the same family. In the same way, the resemblance between modern humans and the earliest humanlike creatures is strong enough to show that these two groups belong to the same family. Members of the human family are called hominids (HOM-uh-nidz).

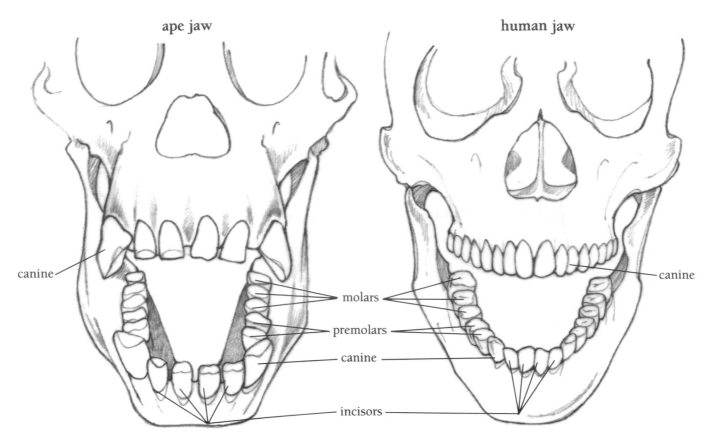

ape jaw   human jaw

canine

molars

premolars

canine

canine

incisors

In some ways early hominids were quite similar to us. They had hominid teeth; their canine teeth were small. And, like all hominids, they had V-shaped jaws. Their hands, feet, and bodies were almost identical to ours. Moreover, they were bipedal: they walked upright on two feet. Hominids are the only creatures who normally walk upright. Monkeys and apes are not hominids. They have long, protruding canines and U-shaped jaws, and they are not normally bipedal. Great apes can walk short distances on their hind legs, but they do not usually do so.

Hominids are either humans, extinct ancestors of humans, or distant cousins of humans. All humans are hominids, but not all hominids are humans.

Nobody knows when the first hominids appeared on earth. We may never know. We know only about those whose fossils have been found, and unfortunately hominid fossils are rare.

Fossils form when an individual is completely buried immediately after death by sand, silt, or volcanic ash. Mineral-rich water seeping through the deposits over thousands of years turns bone into stone. Most fossils are found only after they erode out of cliffs many centuries later. The newly exposed fossils are fragile, and if they are not discovered soon and treated with chemicals they crumble to dust.

The population of ancient hominids was probably never very large, and the bones of only a few turned to stone. Under such circumstances we are very fortunate to know anything at all about our hominid ancestors.

Most people are curious about their ancestry. Some spend many hours in libraries and courthouses digging through old records, searching for information about their great-great-grandparents. Scientists called paleoanthropologists (PAY-lee-o-an-thro-POL-o-gists) spend their lives crawling over ancient hillsides and along modern streams. They dig through rocks and rubble looking for information about the ancestors of the entire human species—evidence that will tell us what these ancestors looked like and when, where, and how they lived.

The task is not an easy one. All of this information has been locked up in the library of time—buried deep in ancient rocks. At this very instant hominid fossils someplace in the world are eroding from the rocks that have preserved them. If they are not found soon, the information they could give us will be gone forever.

A paleoanthropologist's work is a little like trying to solve a mystery or put together a giant jigsaw puzzle with many pieces missing. Still, a bit of evidence here and a few clues there add up to a fairly clear picture.

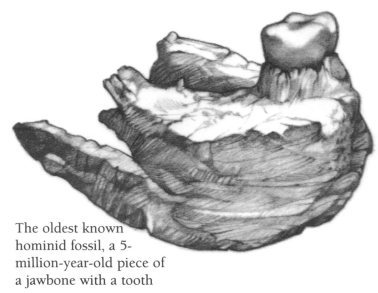

The oldest known hominid fossil, a 5-million-year-old piece of a jawbone with a tooth

Hominid fossils are most often single bones or teeth, which are the most durable parts of the body and therefore the most likely to become fossilized. Only rarely are complete skeletons or skulls found. But bones and teeth can tell us a lot. They are scientific facts—evidence of prehistoric beings.

The oldest hominid fossil found to date is a five-million-year-old piece of a jawbone with a single molar attached. It is too fragmentary to tell us anything about the creature it came from, but it establishes that hominids existed five million years ago. We know the fossil is from a hominid because no other animal has teeth exactly like those of a hominid.

The first evidence of ancient hominids was found less than a hundred years ago. More about human ancestry has been learned in the last ten years than was discovered in the previous ninety put together. There is now enough evidence to prove beyond a doubt that humanlike creatures lived millions of years ago; we have a general picture of what they looked like, how big they were, when and where they lived, and what other animals they lived among.

Just as police officers gather facts at the scene of a crime, paleoanthropologists gather all of the information they can at an archeological site. Since there are no eyewitnesses, they must solve their mysteries using only the evidence they gather. They report their findings so that other scientists can compare the new information with facts they already have. Together they try to figure out what happened at that spot so long ago.

Teeth give clues to the diet of an individual and the age at death. Stone tools indicate something of the user's way of life and suggest that the hand that made them was almost exactly like our own. Bones of other animals found with hominids give clues to the climate of the region. Evidence of camping places suggests where the hominids lived, how they protected themselves from predators, and how many of them traveled together.

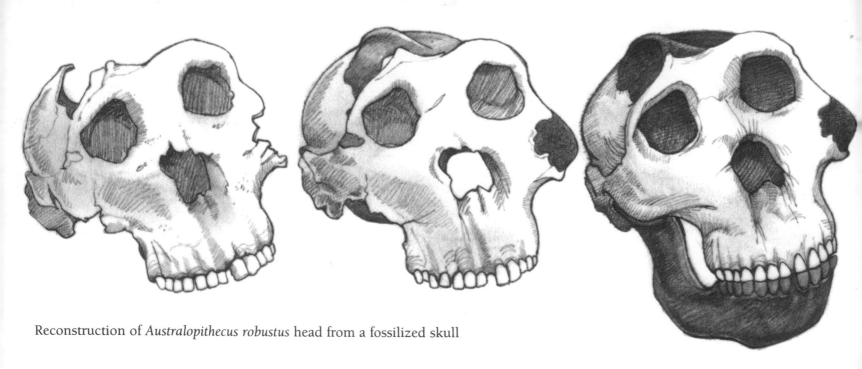

Reconstruction of *Australopithecus robustus* head from a fossilized skull

Scientists spend many hours putting together skeletons and skulls from fragments. Scientific artists make casts of the fossils and attach clay muscles to the casts in places where scars on the bones show muscles were once fastened. Then they add daubs of clay where deposits of fat would normally be. Finally they cover the whole thing with a thin sheet of clay to represent skin. Lips, ears, and a nose are added. Such reconstructions give a good idea of a hominid's appearance. Of course, we still don't know exactly what the individuals looked like, because soft tissue does not fossilize. The nose may have been flatter or the ears larger. We also don't know how hairy the creatures were or what color their skin was. Based on the evidence so carefully gathered by paleoanthropologists, illustrators paint scenes depicting the life of early hominids.

Because of the close similarities between even the earliest hominids and modern humans, scientists often draw upon their knowledge of human development to determine essential facts about their hominid discoveries. For example, scientists estimate the age at which a fossil individual died according to the development of the teeth or of the long bones. Sometimes the amount of fusion that has taken place in the skull bones is a clue to the age of the individual. These ages are only estimates because we do not know for sure that early hominids developed at the same rate as modern humans.

Today scientists can determine fairly accurately how old a fossil is geologically, that is, how long ago it lived. About two hundred years ago the wisest men of Europe thought that humans had been on earth only six thousand years. This knowledge was based on the only evidence they had at the time—the written records of the Hebrews. A hundred years ago scientists thought the earth was sixty-five million years old. Today we know that the earth is many billions of years old and that humans existed much earlier than was thought.

To find the approximate geological age of a fossil, modern scientists measure the amount of radioactive material in rocks found near it. In volcanic materials they can measure the potassium atoms and argon atoms. Potassium decays into argon at a known rate. In 2.1 billion years half of every eighteen potassium atoms will have decayed into eight calcium atoms and one argon atom. The amount of decay is the clue to the age of the lava. For fossils not found with volcanic material, scientists often rely on their knowledge of the age of other animals found with the hominids. Fossils less than fifty thousand years old can be dated by measuring the amount of carbon 14 they contain, or the amount contained in charcoal found with them.

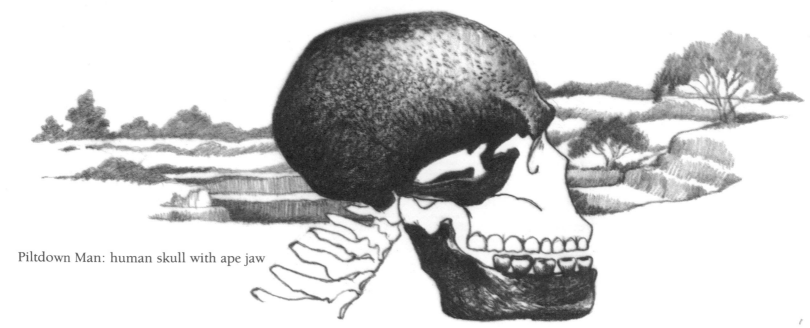

Piltdown Man: human skull with ape jaw

The discovery of ways to date fossils accurately, which happened around 1950, was a turning point in the study of our ancestors. At last scientists could understand how their hominid and mammal finds fit into millions of years of prehistory. Accurate dating also brought many surprises. Hominids were much older than had been suspected. Humans have been on earth at least 150,000 years, and the oldest hominids have been around for more than 4.5 million years.

Scientists today check and double-check new discoveries and theories. Each fossil is dated, and all other bones found with it are carefully catalogued. In the laboratory it is measured, described, and compared to similar fossils. On the basis of these studies, scientists draw conclusions about its origins. This is hard work and may take many years.

At one time scientists were not as careful as they are today. In 1912 a skull like that of a human with a lower jaw like that of an ape was found in a gravel pit near Piltdown, England. Scientists believed it belonged to an ancient human because people of that time expected the earliest human to look like that. They called it "Piltdown Man." However, as new evidence was found, some scientists began to doubt that Piltdown Man was genuine. Finally, in 1955, tests proved that it was indeed a fake. Someone had taken a modern human's skull and attached to it the jawbone of an ape. The bones had been treated with chemicals to make them look ancient.

Though the fraud was embarrassing to scientists, it served a useful purpose. It led to more careful study and classification of fossils. It is unlikely that such a hoax could happen again, because now greater care is taken in studying fossils. Today new theories are based on solid evidence and fairly complete material, instead of on a single bone or tooth.

Also, today's paleoanthropologists enlist the aid of many other scientists. Geologists tell them how old the sites are; ecologists provide information about the environment of the period; climatologists study plant and animal remains and from these determine climatic conditions; zoologists and anthropologists help explain the behavior of animals; chemists and physicists help in dating. Computers are used to make accurate images of fossils still in rocks and of the inside of stone-filled skulls. Satellites equipped with scanning devices assist by locating places where ancient people once lived.

All in all, today is a very exciting time in the study of human fossils. Many more people are working in the field, and new information is discovered every year. It will take time to study and report on all of this new material, but each piece of new evidence will help prove old theories, upset long-held beliefs, or bring about new ones. Whatever is found, you can be sure that it will add to our present knowledge and understanding of hominids. We already know much more about our ancestors than most people realize.

Scientists divide living things into kingdoms called the animal, plant, and protist kingdoms. Kingdoms are divided into smaller groups called classes, families, genera, and species. *Hominidae* is the name of a family in the animal kingdom.

There are two known genera of hominids: *Australopithecus* (aws-TRAH-luh-PITH-uh-kus), the earliest kind, and *Homo* (HO-mo), the genus to which modern humans belong. Although the australopithecines are the oldest hominids we know of today, scientists do not think they are the oldest that ever lived. Perhaps someday something even older will be found.

Australopithecus afarensis

Australopithecus africanus

Australopithecus robustus

Australopithecus boisei

AFRICA

Afar

Omo Valley

Olduvai Gorge

Laetoli

Sterkfontein
Swartkrans
Kromdraai
Taung

Makapansgat

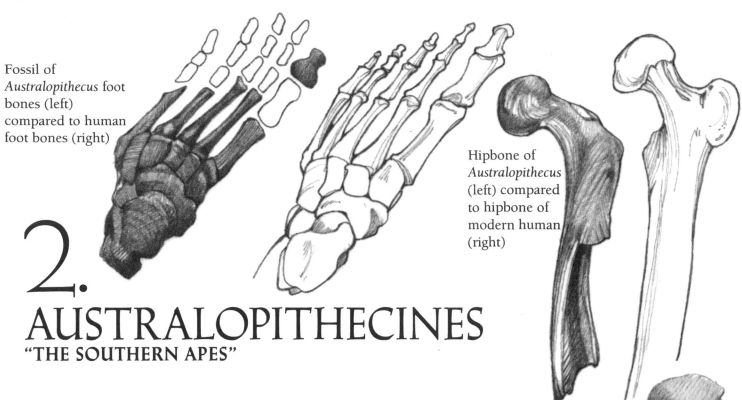

Fossil of *Australopithecus* foot bones (left) compared to human foot bones (right)

Hipbone of *Australopithecus* (left) compared to hipbone of modern human (right)

2. AUSTRALOPITHECINES
"THE SOUTHERN APES"

AUSTRALOPITHECUS IS THE GENUS OF THE OLDEST CREATURES WE know about that clearly belonged to the human family. *Australo* comes from the Latin word meaning "south," and *pithecus* from the Greek word meaning "ape." It was given this name because the first fossil of this genus was an infant's skull found in South Africa. The discoverer was sure it was an early species of hominid, but most scientists of the day thought it was an ape. They thought that it was too old and in the wrong place to be a hominid. They expected the earliest hominid to be found in Asia. Besides, they thought the brain in this skull was too small to be a hominid's. It was not until several other fossils of the same species were found that scientists realized the infant skull was indeed hominid. In spite of its name, an *Australopithecus* was certainly not an ape.

Australopithecines lived in Africa from 4.5 to about 1 million years ago. They were small, ranging from four to five feet in height and weighing between 40 and 120 pounds—about the size of a modern seven- or twelve-year-old child. Males were bigger than females.

Although their arms were somewhat longer and their legs shorter than ours, their skeletons were very similar to ours, and so were their hands and feet. Their knee joints, feet, and pelvises clearly show that they walked on two legs like modern people. Fossilized footprints show that these hominids walked fully upright with no slouching, waddling, or shuffling.

Australopithecus of 3 to 4 million years ago compared to modern *Homo sapiens*

23

From a distance you might not be able to tell the difference between an *Australopithecus* and a modern child. Up close you would see that their heads were different. An australopithecine's head was tilted a little more forward. It had a low, sloping forehead, a small brain cavity, heavy brow ridges, and a receding chin. The jaw was large and protruded somewhat like that of an ape, but was flatter. The back teeth were big and broad, in some species twice as large as modern human teeth, and had thick enamel. The canines and front teeth were small like those of all hominids.

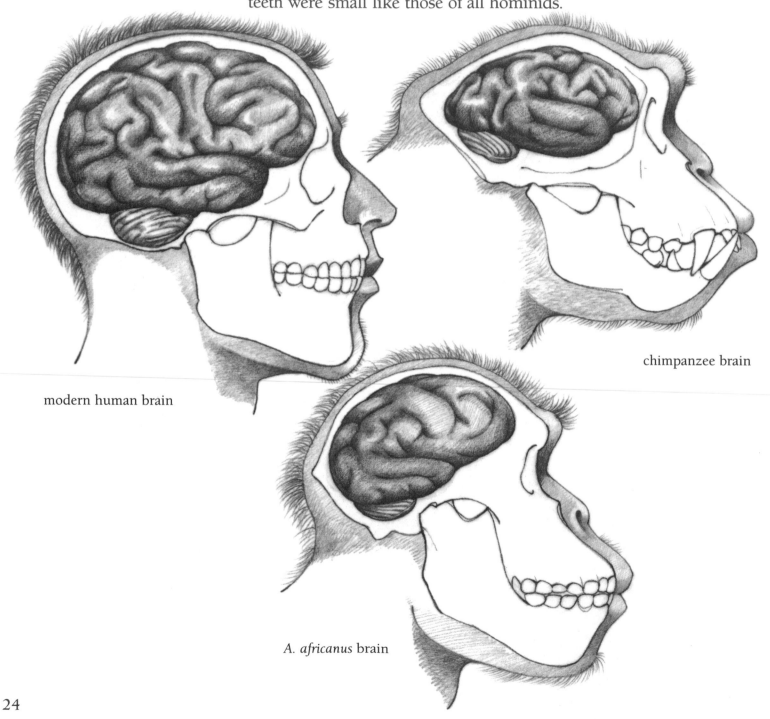

modern human brain

chimpanzee brain

A. africanus brain

The brain of an australopithecine was less than one-third the size of that of a modern human and only a little larger than the brain of a chimpanzee. Scientists were amazed to learn that creatures with such small brains walked upright and had such humanlike bodies.

Because australopithecines had small brains, many people have the idea that these early hominids were stupid and backward. But the fossil evidence shows that they had developed rather sophisticated life-styles millions of years before modern humans appeared on the scene. They most likely were nomadic—they moved constantly in search of food—like primitive tribes of today. They probably had few, if any, possessions. They almost surely shared food with one another. We know that family groups lived in temporary camps, because fossils of entire families have been found together. Perhaps they banded together for protection from large predators.

It is not known if australopithecines could speak. Some scientists believe that they did not have true language such as we do. Others believe they had a primitive language. They surely had vocal communication at least as advanced as that of modern chimpanzees.

There is no evidence that australopithecines made stone tools, so they probably didn't hunt or kill large animals. Wear on their teeth shows that they ate mostly fruit, nuts, roots, and other vegetable food. They probably also ate fish and occasionally may have eaten meat from animals killed by a lion or other predator—similar to the way vultures do today. Some may have eaten eggs and small game. They may have used sticks to dig roots and bones, or river stones as weapons or as hammers to crack nuts. But we have no evidence of that. Sticks are seldom preserved, and there is no way of knowing how (or if) a bone or river stone might have been used.

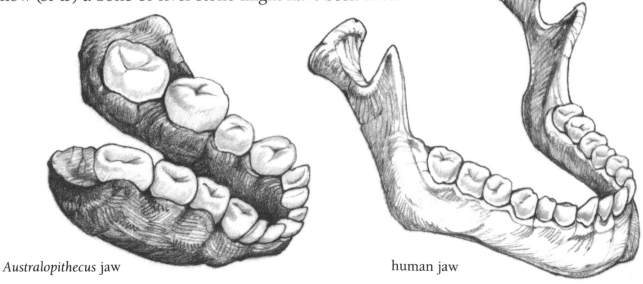

Australopithecus jaw   human jaw

Australopithecines lived in wide-open spaces, called savannas, that looked very much like the African savannas of today. Tall grasses, scattered bushes, and trees dotted the landscape. The climate was dry, with seasonally heavy rainfalls producing flash floods. Many large predators and carnivores lived on the savannas. It was a very dangerous place for these small hominids, who had only their superior intelligence and cooperation for defense. These, however, seem to have been adequate for their survival.

Although some australopithecines may have lived in caves, most of their fossils have been found out in the open in the Great Rift Valley in East Africa. These hominids camped on the shores of a huge, ancient lake or along one of the many rivers or streams that cut through the area. More than a hundred campsites have been found in the gorge. Activities that might have occurred there were not too different from those of today—eating, resting, sleeping, and caring for children.

27

A violent earthquake formed this gorge about a million years ago by splitting the earth apart. It sliced through layers of hominid history, exposing fossils like nuts in a giant layer cake. Heavy rains washed many fossils from the canyon walls. This natural museum of creatures that lived three to four million years ago is an ideal place to find early hominids.

Parts of more than four hundred individual australopithecines have been found altogether, including dozens of skulls and nearly half of a complete skeleton. Alongside the hominid fossils were bones of many other kinds of animals. Familiar birds, monkeys, hyenas, antelopes, lions, bears, giraffes, hippopotamuses, and elephants are abundant. There are also many fossils of huge mammals that are now extinct, including saber-toothed tigers, huge leopards, enormous elephants, and three-toed horses.

Two types of *Australopithecus* lived in Africa: the small, lightly built type (sometimes called "gracile") and the robust type with a thick skull and enormous teeth.

There is some disagreement about how many species of *Australopithecus* there were and whether or not they all belong to the same genus. However, four species are generally accepted: two small types, *Australopithecus afarensis* and *Australopithecus africanus;* and two robust (heavy) types, *Australopithecus robustus* and *Australopithecus boisei.*

During the formation of a valley, layers of earth millions of years old are exposed. Then, through natural erosion, fossils are uncovered and can be found there.

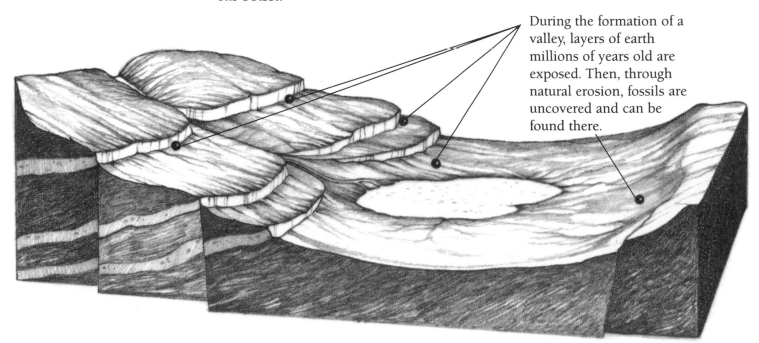

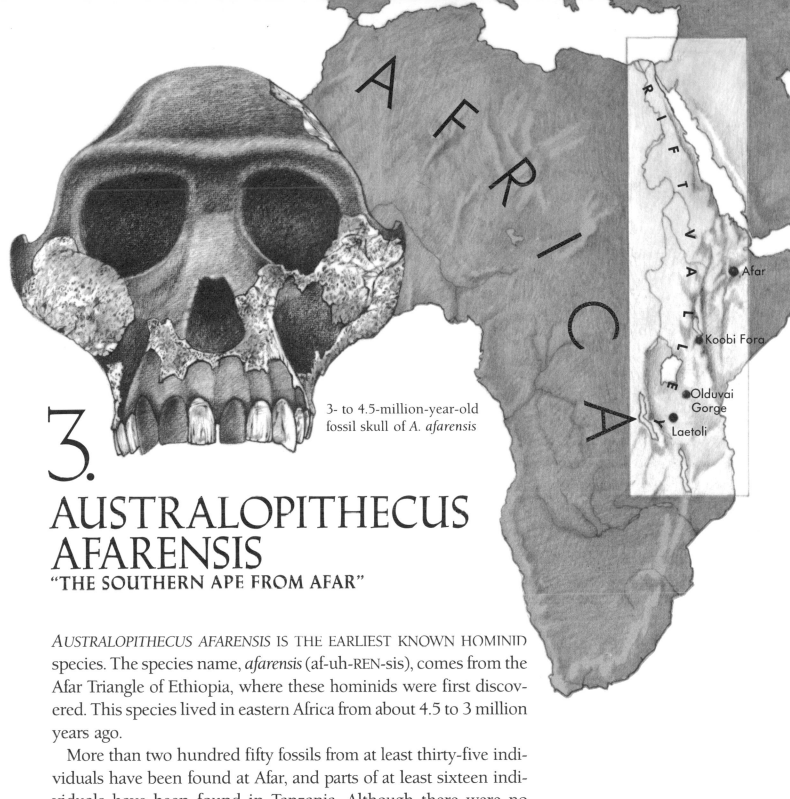

3- to 4.5-million-year-old fossil skull of *A. afarensis*

3.
AUSTRALOPITHECUS AFARENSIS
"THE SOUTHERN APE FROM AFAR"

AUSTRALOPITHECUS AFARENSIS IS THE EARLIEST KNOWN HOMINID species. The species name, *afarensis* (af-uh-REN-sis), comes from the Afar Triangle of Ethiopia, where these hominids were first discovered. This species lived in eastern Africa from about 4.5 to 3 million years ago.

More than two hundred fifty fossils from at least thirty-five individuals have been found at Afar, and parts of at least sixteen individuals have been found in Tanzania. Although there were no complete skeletons, almost every bone of the body is represented, including more than a dozen bones from one foot.

No complete skull has been found yet, but a scientist pieced together parts of three separate skulls to form a whole one. It took him several months of hard work to complete the task. The day

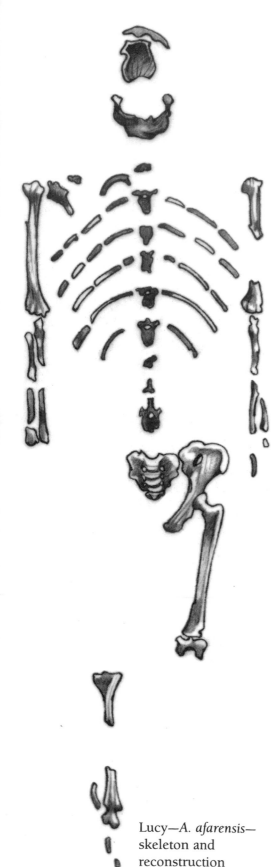

Lucy—*A. afarensis*—
skeleton and
reconstruction

after he finished, the skull rolled off the table and shattered to bits. The devastated scientist had to put the skull back together again, because it was important. Without it there was no way of knowing what *A. afarensis* looked like.

The most famous *A. afarensis,* and the most complete australopithecine found to date, is a partial skeleton of an adult nicknamed "Lucy." The shape of the pelvis shows that Lucy was a female; the pelvis is remarkably similar to that of a modern human female. Scientists think that Lucy was about twenty years old when she died, because she had already cut her wisdom teeth but they show very little wear.

The second most important *A. afarensis* fossil discovery was a family group. At least thirteen individuals—nine adults (males and females) and four children—died together, possibly in a flash flood. The development of the children's teeth indicates that they were all under five years of age.

The *A. afarensis* were small. Males were 5 feet tall and weighed about 120 pounds. Females were from 3.5 to 4 feet tall and weighed about 60 pounds—about the size of a six- or seven-year-old child of today. Although short, these creatures were probably powerful. Markings on their thick bones show that they had heavy muscles. Their bodies were extraordinarily like those of humans, except that their arms were a little longer for the size of their bodies than those of modern humans, and their legs were shorter. The hands and feet were almost exactly like those of modern humans.

Their heads, however, were primitive—small and somewhat apelike, with large thrusting jaws, small chins, and small brains. The brain of the largest could have been no larger than a softball, about 450 cubic centimeters (not quite one pint). A large ape has a brain that measures 400 cubic centimeters.

We don't know how hairy *A. afarensis* were, nor the color of their hair. We also don't know the color of their skin, but it was probably black, since they lived in the tropics where dark skin is needed to protect against the strong rays of the sun.

The feet, pelvis, knees, and thighs plainly show that *A. afarensis* were bipedal. But an even more exciting bit of evidence, a seventy-seven-foot trail of footprints, shows that they had a fully human stride. They did not shuffle or waddle. The fifty footprints, which were discovered in Tanzania, had been made by two hominids traveling north about 3.7 million years ago. One of the hominids was smaller than the other. It is not certain whether the two were traveling together. The smaller individual's tracks are slightly to one side of the other's. At one point the smaller hominid had stopped and turned, perhaps to look at something, before going on. The prints look exactly like human footprints that might be seen on any beach today, except that they had been made in damp volcanic ash that was covered over almost immediately with new ash. These footprints prove that these hominids walked just the way we do and probably had been doing so for a long time. The only known hominid 3.7 million years old is *A. afarensis,* so it is assumed that these hominids made the tracks.

Though the teeth of A. *afarensis* were somewhat like those of apes, they resemble human teeth in size, enamel, and shape. The canines were small, and there were small gaps between them and the incisors. The molars were larger than an ape's and were capped with thicker enamel, probably because A. *afarensis* ate lots of heavy vegetable fiber. Examinations of the teeth under an electron microscope reveal that they were probably used to chew both vegetables and meat.

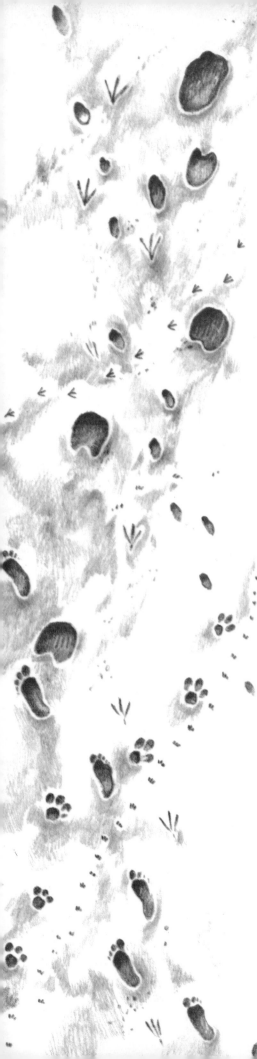

There is no evidence that A. *afarensis* made or used tools. This does not mean they did not. Even chimpanzees of today use grass stems and twigs as tools. These hominids may have used sticks or bones to dig roots or tubers. They may have thrown rounded stones at predators.

The fossil evidence does not tell us how these hominids lived. The discovery of a family buried together indicates that they lived in family groups, but there is no evidence of a home base. They may have banded together for protection and to find food. This would have made it easier to find enough food to feed everyone and to catch prey. A. *afarensis* were probably nomadic—traveling about from one food source to another. They probably did not own any possessions.

Fossil pollen found with the Afar fossils shows that A. *afarensis* lived in a high tropical region of lush woodlands on the fringe of the savannas. Winding rivers and many lakes cut through the area. As many as ten volcanoes may have been erupting there at one time.

Many animals we know today lived in the region. Some of their tracks were left in the volcanic ash along with the hominid footprints. Elephants, guinea fowl, giraffes, bears, three-toed horses, and ostriches had crossed the ash either just before the hominids or just after. Owls, cheetahs, giraffes, rhinoceroses, monkeys, rodents, wild pigs, hyenas, and now-extinct elephant-like creatures with tusks in their lower jaws are also known to have lived there. The Tanzania area was drier then than it is today. This shows that the earliest hominids were able to adapt to different climates.

Over millions of years, silt from streams filled the lakes and covered the bones with hundreds of feet of sand and clay, which then turned to stone. Present-day rivers and streams have cut deep channels through these deposits, exposing the fossils of the creatures that lived on the shores of the ancient lake.

The most important of these to us is *Australopithecus afarensis*. This is the hominid generally considered to be the ancestor of all other australopithecines and perhaps of *Homo sapiens* (modern humans).

Some scientists believe that A. *afarensis* may be a primitive race of *Australopithecus africanus;* most, however, think that it is a separate hominid species.

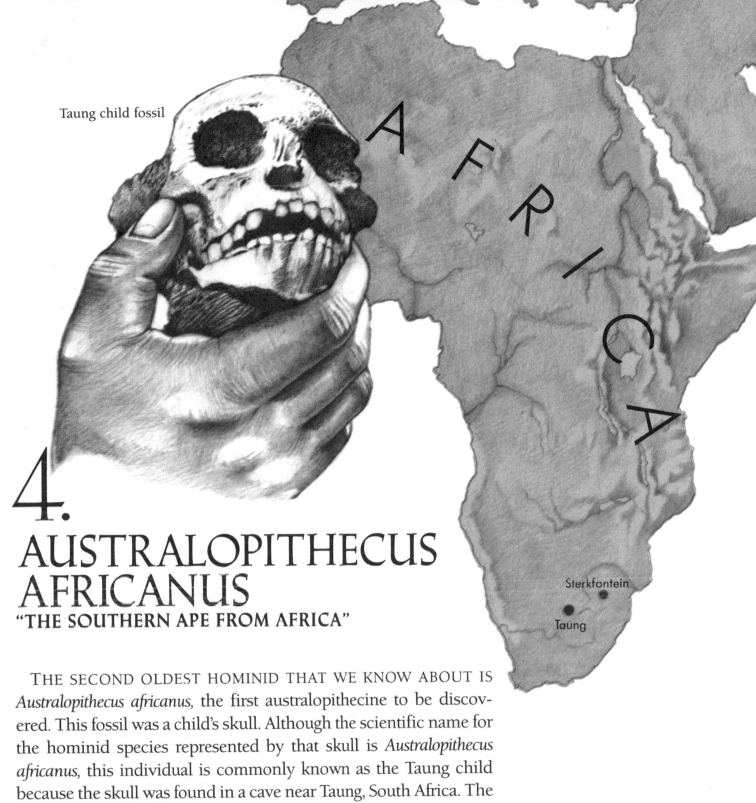

Taung child fossil

AFRICA

Sterkfontein

Taung

4.
AUSTRALOPITHECUS AFRICANUS
"THE SOUTHERN APE FROM AFRICA"

THE SECOND OLDEST HOMINID THAT WE KNOW ABOUT IS *Australopithecus africanus,* the first australopithecine to be discovered. This fossil was a child's skull. Although the scientific name for the hominid species represented by that skull is *Australopithecus africanus,* this individual is commonly known as the Taung child because the skull was found in a cave near Taung, South Africa. The species name, *africanus* (af-ruh-KAN-us), comes from the country where the fossil was found.

The Taung child was originally thought to be about six years old when it died, because it had already cut all of its baby teeth and its first molars were just coming through. However, growth rings on the teeth indicate that it may have been only three years old.

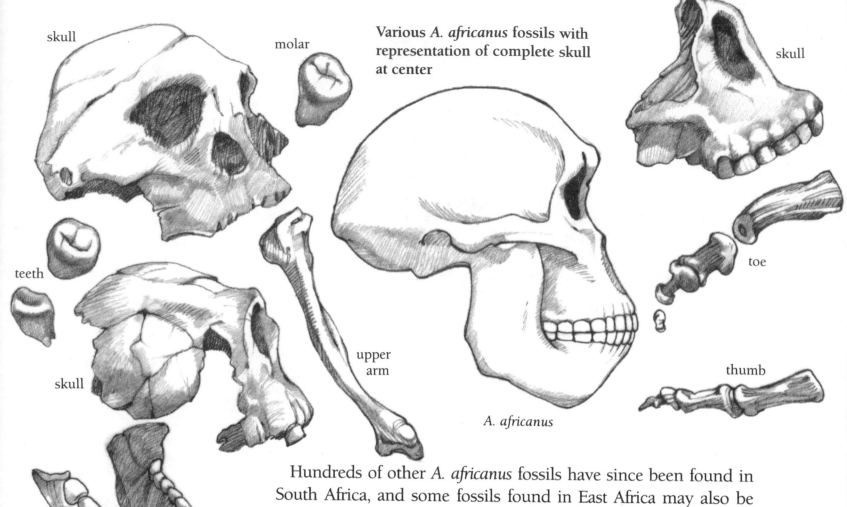

skull

molar

Various *A. africanus* fossils with representation of complete skull at center

skull

teeth

skull

toe

upper arm

thumb

A. africanus

jaw

pelvis

Hundreds of other *A. africanus* fossils have since been found in South Africa, and some fossils found in East Africa may also be *A. africanus*. This hominid lived from about three million to two million years ago. The exact age of the oldest known fossil, however, is in question.

A complete skeleton of *A. africanus* has not yet been found, but enough is known to give us a pretty good idea of this hominid's size and general appearance. Parts of at least forty-seven individuals of all ages and both sexes have been found. These include hundreds of jaws and teeth, part of a hand with a thumb like a human's, five pelvises (one complete with most of the spine above it), a fragment of upper arm and shoulder, a wrist, a thigh, ribs, and some knee joints.

Several nearly complete skulls have also been found. Some of them contained stone casts of the inside, showing the shape and size of the brain. The brain capacity of *A. africanus* ranged from 450 cubic centimeters to 500 cubic centimeters—about one pint, a little larger than that of a gorilla, but less than half the size of a modern human brain. Though the brain was small, it was like a human's in shape, more rounded and less elongated than that of a gorilla.

A. afarensis

A. africanus

modern H. sapiens

One nearly perfect skull, discovered with a female pelvis, was dubbed "Mrs. Ples" by its finder. A recent CAT scan (computer-assisted tomography, sometimes called a CT scan—a special kind of X-ray) of this skull and its middle and inner ear canals shows that the head was probably carried farther forward and at a greater angle than the head of a modern human.

In some ways A. africanus is similar to A. afarensis. Both were small, with slender bodies and lightweight bones. A. africanus was about the same size as A. afarensis—about four feet in height and seventy-five pounds in weight. However, the teeth of A. africanus are quite different from those of A. afarensis. Although the canine teeth are about the same size, the molars of A. africanus are larger, about twice the size of a modern human's molars, and the enamel on them is extremely thick. The incisors are smaller than those of A. afarensis.

modern
H. sapiens
molar

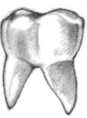

A. africanus
molar

The face of A. africanus was small and shaped somewhat like an ape's. It had a low, rounded forehead and a hint of a muzzle, but no jutting chin or great eyebrow ridges. The skull was high and rounded. The skeleton was quite similar to, though not exactly like, that of a modern human.

37

Little is known about the way these hominids lived. We know that they had a short life span. More than a third of those whose fossils have been found had died before they reached adulthood. Their average age was twenty-three years.

Although most of the fossils of *A. africanus* have been found in caves in South Africa, these hominids apparently did not live in the caves, as scientists originally thought. Many of the skulls were crushed, and it was once believed that they had been bashed in by other *A. africanus*. Five hundred bones of other animals were also found in the caves, and it was supposed that *A. africanus* or another hominid had killed and eaten them. This led to the idea that these hominids were vicious killers. However, recent research shows that the skulls had been crushed by the weight of a hundred feet of sediment piled on top of them, and the bones had been carried there by predators, probably leopards or hyenas.

Although *A. africanus* did not eat the animals in the cave, they probably occasionally ate small game. Their teeth indicate that they ate some meat—possibly small animals, fish, lizards, and eggs—as well as hard fruit and other tough plant food. They probably hunted and foraged in small bands.

38

Food was plentiful. The climate of both South Africa and eastern Africa was about the same then as it is now. These areas were on the fringe of a desert and were probably dry, grassy plains with straw-colored, waist-high grass. Scattered bushes and trees grew near swamps and waterholes and along the winding rivers that emptied into large lakes. Fossil pollen shows that oak, holly, pine, juniper, and palm trees grew near the streams and lakes.

Relatively few plains animals were represented by the animal bones found in the caves with the hominids. This seems to indicate that the South African group of these little hominids lived in brushy areas along streams and near lakes where they could find more protection from predators. The East African group also lived along lakes and streams.

A. africanus may have been preyed on by many predators. Lions and saber-toothed cats as well as leopards and hyenas lived in both regions. Lakes were full of fish and seabirds, and they may have been a primary source of food as well as water. Flamingos and crocodiles lived along the edges of the lakes, and monkeys played in the trees nearby. Rats and moles burrowed in the ground. Strange animals, now extinct—three-toed horses, elephants with two tusks in the lower jaw and two in the upper jaw, gigantic antlered giraffes, and giant baboons—roamed the grasslands along with hippos, wild pigs, antelope, and hyraxes.

39

Australopithecus africanus was a very successful species. These hominids had developed stable life-styles and had adapted well to their environment. They had spread over wide areas and existed for about a million years before becoming extinct. It is not known if they shared food, or if they made tools, although their hands were perfectly capable of making and using tools. Some believe that they may have used bone tools—bones that seem to have been used as digging sticks have been found—but this cannot be positively proven.

Almost all scientists agree that *A. africanus* was a hominid, but they disagree over whether it was a direct ancestor of modern humans. Until the discovery of *A. afarensis* it was assumed to be. Even though *A. afarensis* is older, its teeth seem to have more characteristics in common with those of modern humans than do those of *A. africanus*. For this reason, many scientists now think *A. africanus* was not ancestral to modern humans but a member of another branch on the family tree—a sort of great-great-great-great-aunt. It was almost certainly ancestral to the robust australopithecines.

A. africanus digging roots

42

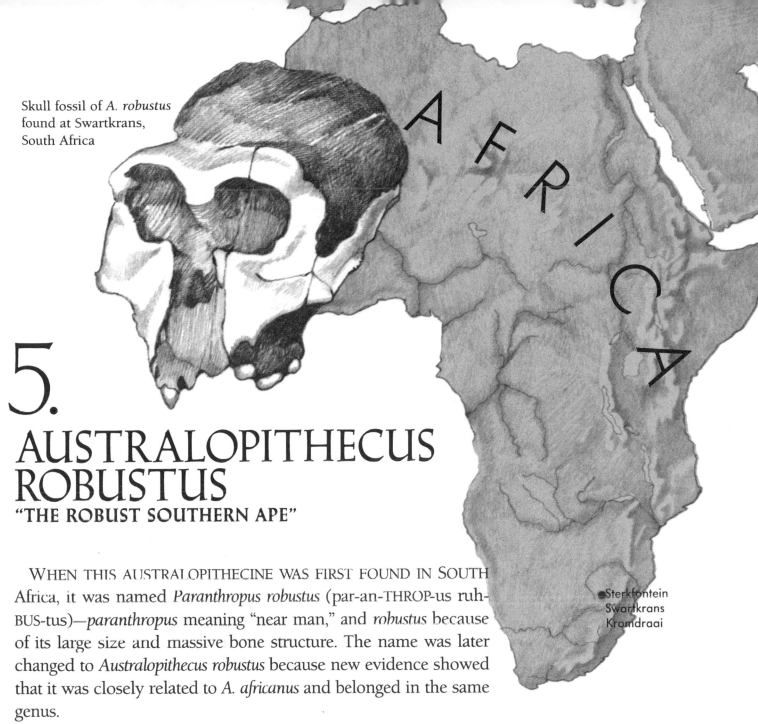

Skull fossil of *A. robustus* found at Swartkrans, South Africa

5. AUSTRALOPITHECUS ROBUSTUS
"THE ROBUST SOUTHERN APE"

Sterkfontein
Swartkrans
Kromdraai

WHEN THIS AUSTRALOPITHECINE WAS FIRST FOUND IN SOUTH Africa, it was named *Paranthropus robustus* (par-an-THROP-us ruh-BUS-tus)—*paranthropus* meaning "near man," and *robustus* because of its large size and massive bone structure. The name was later changed to *Australopithecus robustus* because new evidence showed that it was closely related to *A. africanus* and belonged in the same genus.

A. robustus was quite similar to *A. africanus* in several ways. It stood fully erect, walked bipedally, and had a small brain with a cranial capacity of about 500 cubic centimeters (a little over a pint), about the same as that of *A. africanus.* The arms were long and the feet and hands were basically like a human's. But its bones were much more massive than those of the smaller, lighter-weight australopithecines. It was also taller and heavier. This stocky australopithecine was 4.5 to 5 feet tall and weighed about one hundred pounds. Females were shorter and less robust than males.

The head, too, was very different from that of *A. africanus*. It was large. The face was long and flat with massive jaws and heavy brow ridges. The forehead was extremely short, and the top of the head was low.

Many *A. robustus* had extremely wide, flaring cheekbones. In addition, males had a high bony crest that ran along the top of the skull from front to back. It is believed that this bony ridge and the wide cheekbones had developed to provide a place for the attachment of the very strong muscles needed to work the massive jaws and huge teeth.

A. robustus had enormous molars and premolars. They were bigger, broader, and more heavily enameled than those of *A. africanus*. They were twice as large as ours. The grinding surface of some of the molars was about the size of a dime. The incisors and front teeth, however, were about the same size as those of a modern human.

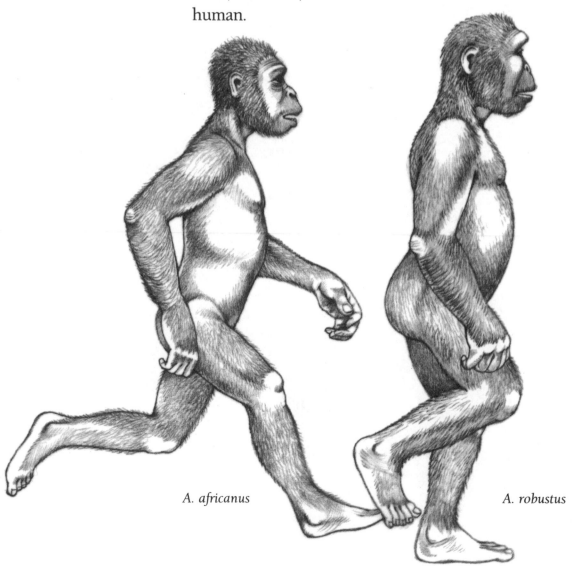

A. africanus   A. robustus

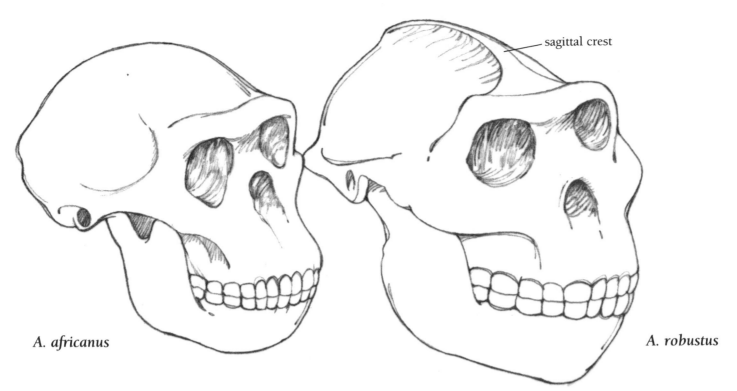

A. africanus

sagittal crest

A. robustus

Scientists believe that the teeth of these burly creatures grew so large because they ate large quantities of vegetable material. It was once thought that they ate nothing but tough, coarse roots; hard fruit; stalks; and grass. But recently it has been suggested that their food was not necessarily tough; it may have been of such poor quality that they had to eat a great deal of it. Studies of the teeth show that A. robustus probably did not eat grass or roots at all. They may not have eaten much fruit, either, because not many fruits grew where they lived. There were few trees of any kind, except along the streams.

Unlike those of A. africanus, A. robustus fossils have been found only in limestone caves in South Africa. These caves are near those where A. africanus was found but are of a more recent age. The earliest known A. robustus is about two million years old.

Bones of other animals found in the same caves suggest that the area was considerably drier during this period than it was when A. africanus lived. Many species of plains animals were among those found. There were bones of antelopes, wildebeests, springbok, hartebeests, and gazelles. Such a large number of plains animals indicates that the area was an open savanna, probably much like it is today. Fossil pollen shows that the vegetation was mostly tall grasses.

Comparison of gracile and robust types of australopithecines. Note larger jaws and teeth and sagittal crest of A. robustus.

A complete skeleton of *A. robustus* has not yet been found. But parts of at least 134 individuals—ranging from infants to adults—were found in just two caves. Most are craniums and parts of skulls, including palates, jaws, and hundreds of teeth. However, wrists, elbows, arm and leg bones, hand and finger bones, ankles, hipbones, and vertebrae have also been recovered. And more fossils are discovered almost daily as scientists continue to search these caves.

Since these hominids apparently did not make stone tools, there is not much evidence to suggest the way they lived. They may have hunted small game—lizards, eggs, and such. But like *A. africanus,* they were obviously the hunted more often than the hunters. More than half of those that have been found died before they reached adulthood. Their average age was eighteen. All of their bones and most of the animal bones found with them had been gnawed by large predators such as saber-toothed cats, hyenas, or leopards.

47

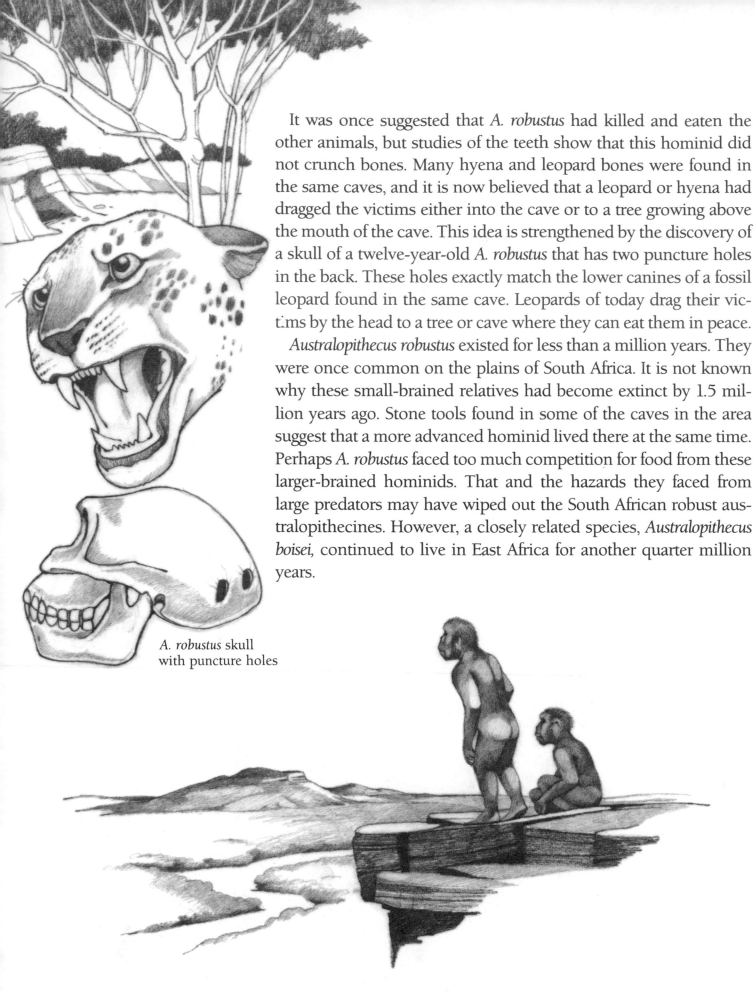

It was once suggested that *A. robustus* had killed and eaten the other animals, but studies of the teeth show that this hominid did not crunch bones. Many hyena and leopard bones were found in the same caves, and it is now believed that a leopard or hyena had dragged the victims either into the cave or to a tree growing above the mouth of the cave. This idea is strengthened by the discovery of a skull of a twelve-year-old *A. robustus* that has two puncture holes in the back. These holes exactly match the lower canines of a fossil leopard found in the same cave. Leopards of today drag their victims by the head to a tree or cave where they can eat them in peace.

Australopithecus robustus existed for less than a million years. They were once common on the plains of South Africa. It is not known why these small-brained relatives had become extinct by 1.5 million years ago. Stone tools found in some of the caves in the area suggest that a more advanced hominid lived there at the same time. Perhaps *A. robustus* faced too much competition for food from these larger-brained hominids. That and the hazards they faced from large predators may have wiped out the South African robust australopithecines. However, a closely related species, *Australopithecus boisei*, continued to live in East Africa for another quarter million years.

A. robustus skull
with puncture holes

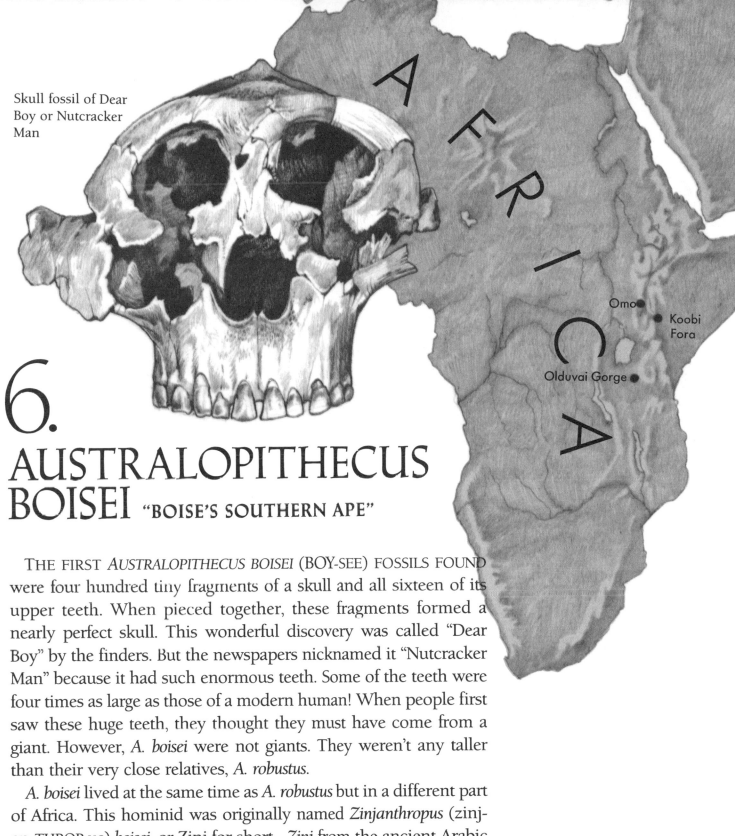

Skull fossil of Dear
Boy or Nutcracker
Man

A F R I C A

Omo

Koobi
Fora

Olduvai Gorge

6.
AUSTRALOPITHECUS
BOISEI "BOISE'S SOUTHERN APE"

THE FIRST *AUSTRALOPITHECUS BOISEI* (BOY-SEE) FOSSILS FOUND
were four hundred tiny fragments of a skull and all sixteen of its
upper teeth. When pieced together, these fragments formed a
nearly perfect skull. This wonderful discovery was called "Dear
Boy" by the finders. But the newspapers nicknamed it "Nutcracker
Man" because it had such enormous teeth. Some of the teeth were
four times as large as those of a modern human! When people first
saw these huge teeth, they thought they must have come from a
giant. However, *A. boisei* were not giants. They weren't any taller
than their very close relatives, *A. robustus*.

   A. boisei lived at the same time as *A. robustus* but in a different part
of Africa. This hominid was originally named *Zinjanthropus* (zinj-
an-THROP-us) *boisei*, or Zinj for short—*Zinj* from the ancient Arabic
word for East Africa, where the first specimen was found, and
anthropus from the Greek word for "man." *Boisei* is in honor of
Charles Boise of London, a benefactor of the finder.

Comparison of tooth and jaw sizes

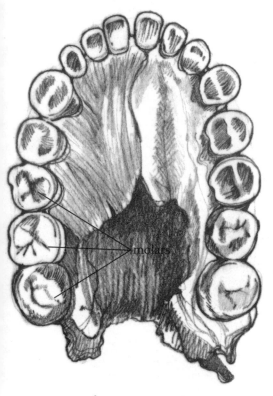

A. *boisei* (Nutcracker Man)
upper teeth

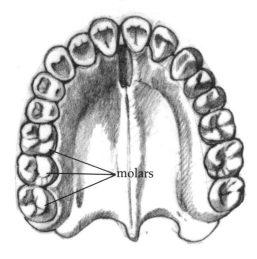

modern *H. sapiens*
upper teeth

Until recently some scientists thought that *A. boisei* and *A. robustus* were variations of the same species. Others thought that *A. boisei* had descended from *A. robustus*. Now we know that *A. boisei* is indeed a different species and could not have descended from *A. robustus*. The discovery in Kenya of a new skull, catalogued as KNM-WT 17000 but popularly called "the black skull," leaves little doubt of that.

The finder thinks that this 2.5-million-year-old skull was a very early *A. boisei*. However, some scientists believe the black skull belonged to a different species. They suggest that it was an *A. aethiopicus* (ee-thee-o-PIC-us), the name given to a similar-age lower jaw first found in Ethiopia. The black skull has no lower jaw, so there is no way to prove this one way or the other.

This new skull is important, but it does not solve the mystery of just how the australopithecines were related. If it is indeed an early *A. boisei*, then *A. boisei* could not have descended from *A. africanus*, because both existed at the same time. It may have descended from *A. afarensis*. A great deal more study will need to be done before we can fully understand the australopithecine lineage.

The black skull is much older than any known *A. robustus*. Although its face was more advanced (it was flatter or more dishlike) than that of *A. robustus*, its brain capacity was smaller.

A. boisei were much more massively built than *A. robustus*. Although they were about the same height—between four and five feet tall—*A. boisei* weighed about 120 pounds. Females were shorter and less robust than males. The skull was also thicker and heavier than that of *A. robustus*. In fact, the *A. boisei* skull is the largest and most robust hominid skull known. As in all australopithecines, the cranium was flat and the braincase small, averaging 534 cubic centimeters in volume—barely over a pint. The 2.5-million-year-old skull had a brain capacity of only 410 cubic centimeters—smaller even than that of *A. afarensis*. It is because of this and other minor differences that some scientists suggest that the new skull should be placed in a separate species. Wherever it ends up, it is clearly an early ancestor of *A. boisei*.

The *A. boisei* face was huge. It was long, flat, and wide, with an enormous mouth and immense, thick, powerful jaws. Like *A. robustus*, males of this species had very wide cheekbones and a ridge, or crest, running down the middle of the cranium. These cheekbones and crests were even more massive than those of *A. robustus* because they anchored thicker and more powerful jaw muscles.

A. boisei's molars were twice as large as those of *A. robustus* (a molar in the new skull was five times larger than a modern human's). These millstone-like teeth are up to one inch front to back—twice as big as a postage stamp. The premolars were also unusually large and molar-like. The incisors and canines were tiny in comparison—about the same size as a modern human's.

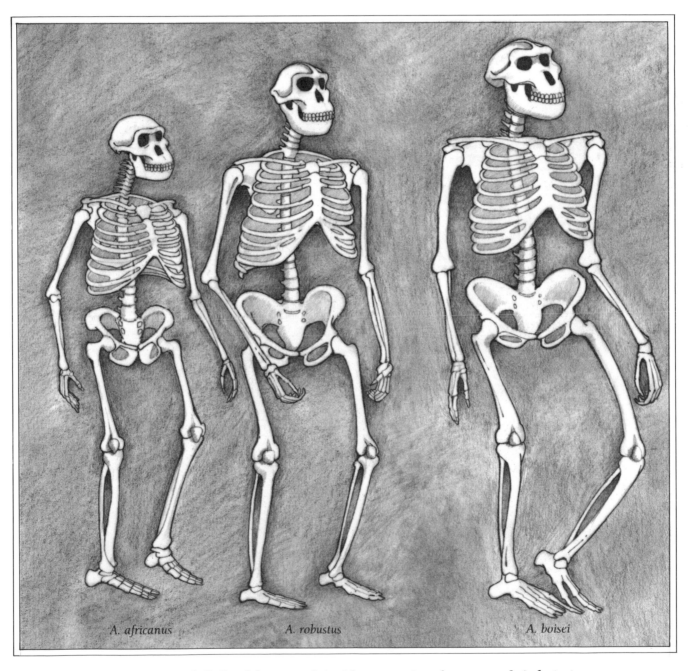

A. africanus   *A. robustus*   *A. boisei*

Comparison of skeletal frames of *A. Africanus*, *A. robustus*, and *A. boisei*

A. *boisei* fossils have been found in several parts of East Africa—Kenya, Tanzania, and Ethiopia. They lived from a little more than 2 million years ago to about 1.4 million years ago. Not only did they live before A. *robustus*, they continued to live after A. *robustus* had died out.

Geologically, Dear Boy was 1.8 million years old. He was the first fossil to be accurately dated by the potassium/argon method. Scientists think that Dear Boy was about eighteen years old when he died. His wisdom teeth had come through but showed no wear, and the skull bones had already fused, which indicates that he was probably older than sixteen.

Another complete A. *boisei* skull, three partial skulls, several skull fragments, and teeth and jaws have been found, as well as arm and leg bones and an ankle bone. Four jaws found in Java and originally named *Meganthropus* (meg-an-THROP-us) may also be those of A. *boisei*.

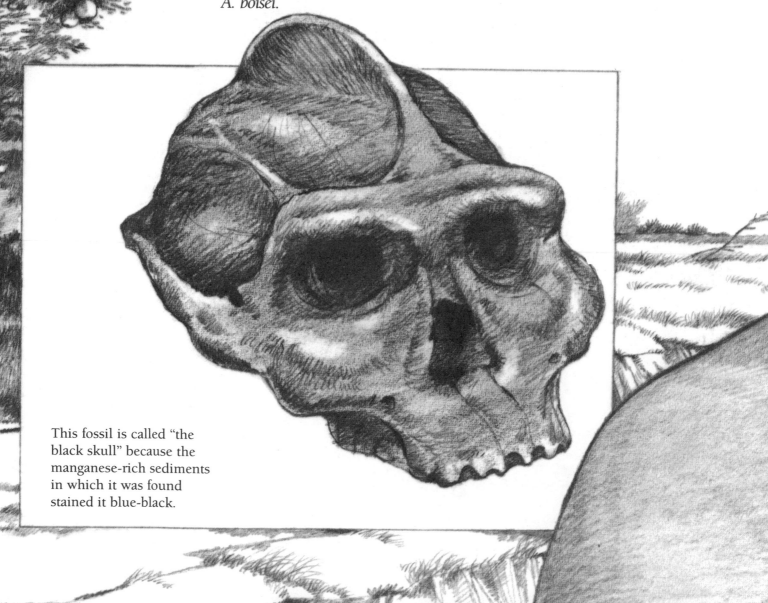

This fossil is called "the black skull" because the manganese-rich sediments in which it was found stained it blue-black.

A. boisei

Eastern Africa must have been a very interesting place for these early hominids to live. The region was mostly a thornbush savanna, probably somewhat lusher than it is today. The plants were similar to today's. Fruiting trees and bushes grew close to the many streams and rivers that fed the ancient lakes. Plains lay to the west and volcanoes to the east. As many as a hundred species of animal and bird life that are now extinct, including prehistoric pigs as big as rhinoceroses with tusks as long as an elephant's, six-foot-tall sheep with five-yard hornspans, a short-necked giraffe with antlers like those of a modern moose, giant baboons bigger than a modern gorilla, and twelve-foot ostriches, lived in the area. It was also very dangerous because there were many large predators—leopards, hyenas, wild dogs, and saber-toothed tigers.

The climate was warm, about the same as it is today, but probably somewhat wetter. There seem to have been seasonably heavy rainfalls.

We know very little about the life-style of these hominids. It was probably much like that of *A. africanus. A boisei* may have dug with sticks and hammered with stones, but there is no evidence of this.

There is evidence that they suffered from diseases. The teeth of Dear Boy suggest that he may have been a sickly child. The enamel of permanent teeth builds up layer by layer and all illnesses retard the growth of enamel, showing up as tiny hollows in the surface.

This child had deep hollows, indicating that he had a disease that lasted many months. He had also suffered three other major attacks of ill health at the ages of two, three, and four and a half. He could have had amoebic dysentery, malaria, or typhoid—all diseases known to have existed at that time—or malnutrition.

A. boisei probably did not eat much red meat. Their teeth could not have torn the skin or fur from a rabbit or squirrel. Scientists believe their diet was mostly vegetable food—roots, tubers, and some fruit. Most of the fossil teeth had been worn flat on top, which suggests that these hominids chewed a lot of tough fiber. The extremely heavy jaw muscles also indicate this. However, there are indications that they sometimes ate insects and small animals—birds, rodents, snakes, and lizards.

Dear Boy's skull was found in a campsite with stone tools, but scientists do not believe that *A. boisei* made these tools. By this time there were other hominids in East Africa—a big-brained species called *Homo habilis* (HO-mo HAB-uh-lis). It is suspected that they were the ones who made the tools.

Why *A. boisei* became extinct is not known. They had lived successfully for more than a million years—from at least 2.25 million years to 1.2 million years ago. They lived with both *A. robustus* and *Homo habilis* for half a million years until those two died out. Then *A. boisei* continued to coexist with an even bigger-brained species for another twenty thousand years.

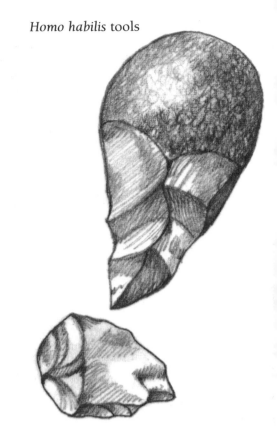

Homo habilis tools

Homo habilis

Homo erectus

Homo sapiens neanderthalensis

Homo sapiens sapiens (Cro-Magnon)

7.
THE GENUS HOMO
"HUMANKIND"

SOMETIME BETWEEN 2.5 AND 2 MILLION YEARS AGO ONE GROUP OF hominids discovered how to make tools from stone. With these tools hominids could harvest and prepare plant foods more efficiently and could cut skins and large chunks of meat from animal carcasses. This made it possible for them to eat more meat. As they did so, their brains grew larger. This set these hominids apart from the australopithecines.

Scientists place these toolmaking hominids in a different genus, the genus *Homo.* The name comes from the Greek word *homo,* meaning "human or mankind." To be classed as *Homo,* a hominid must have a large brain—a cranial capacity of at least 750 cubic centimeters (a little more than a pint and a half)—and it must have made tools.

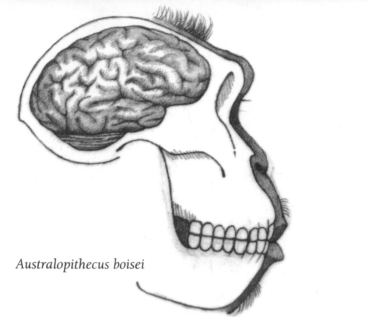

Australopithecus boisei

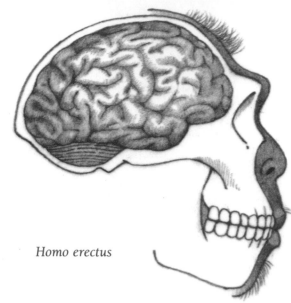

Homo erectus

Other animals sometimes use objects as tools, but members of the genus *Homo* are the only animals that alter natural objects for a particular use and make tools to a regular pattern. They are also the only animals that use one tool to make another. And they are the only animals whose survival is dependent upon this ability.

Most scientists think that the genus *Homo* developed from an *Australopithecus.* But not everyone agrees. Some believe that someday a large-brained species as old as or older than the australopithecines will be found.

Early *Homo* species were more similar in appearance to the lightweight australopithecines than to modern humans. They were about the same size, around four feet tall; their heads were small; and they were probably hairier than modern people. But they were different from the australopithecines in a number of ways. The most important difference was the larger brain capacity. The smallest *Homo* skull has a cranial capacity of 750 cubic centimeters. The largest australopithecine brain was 624 cubic centimeters.

As the *Homo* brain expanded, the skull became thinner and more rounded instead of thick and flat like those of the australopithecines. Although the brows of early species remained heavy, their foreheads and jaws became flatter. Their jaws also became wider, allowing room for larger tongue muscles, making speech possible.

Homo teeth were smaller than those of *Australopithecus,* and the molars were shaped differently. Instead of being wide, they were long and narrow like ours. The hipbones and upper leg bones were also different from those of *Australopithecus.*

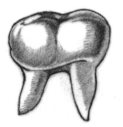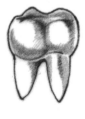

Australopithecus   Homo molar
molar

Another important difference between *Homo* and *Australopithecus* was in the way they lived. We still know very little about the earliest *Homo* species. But we know more about their life-styles than we do about those of the australopithecines. Although fewer *Homo* fossils have been found than australopithecine fossils, a great many of their camping sites have been discovered. Every known *Homo* species has been found with tools of some kind and also with animal bones. Each species made tools of a particular kind.

Finding tools with animal bones or other objects is almost as important as finding the fossils themselves. To a trained scientist these finds tell a story. They indicate that these hominids made tools from stone and used them to cut meat from large animals. We know what kinds of meat the hominids ate and how they butchered it. We also know that they cut skin and tendons from the bones. The marks of their knives can be seen on the bones.

Stone scraper

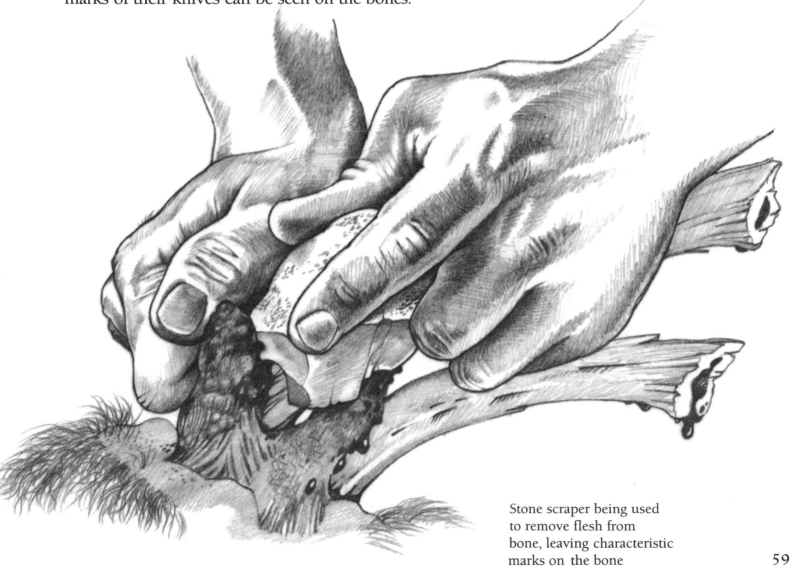

Stone scraper being used to remove flesh from bone, leaving characteristic marks on the bone

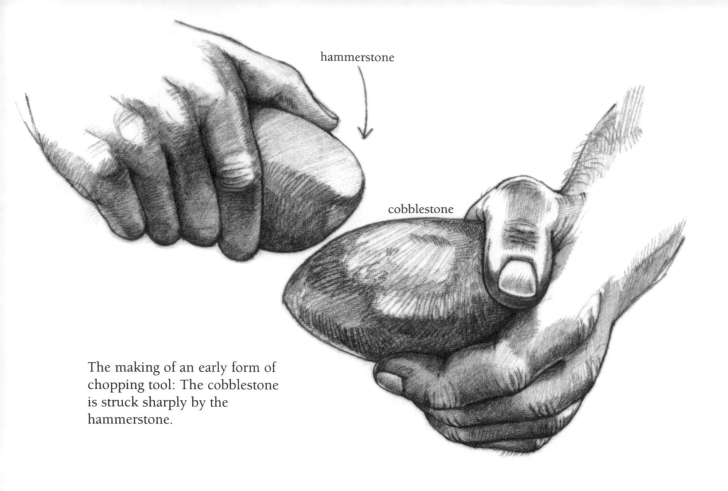

hammerstone

cobblestone

The making of an early form of chopping tool: The cobblestone is struck sharply by the hammerstone.

At first they apparently scavenged for their meat. That is, they ate meat from animals killed by other carnivores. Their simple stone tools were not adequate for killing large animals. Later they learned to drive animals into bogs and butcher them there.

Their first tools were very simple—razor-sharp stone flakes knocked from larger volcanic rocks. They seem to have been used only for cutting when harvesting plant food or for butchering meat. Some apparently were made at the place of a large animal kill. Material for making them had to be carried to the spot. Sometimes the hominid traveled long distances to obtain the material.

As *Homo* brains grew larger, the toolmakers became more skillful. Their stone tools became more intricate and complex, and their "tool kit" (the number of tools manufactured) became larger. Some of these hominids probably started trading tools or the materials from which they were made.

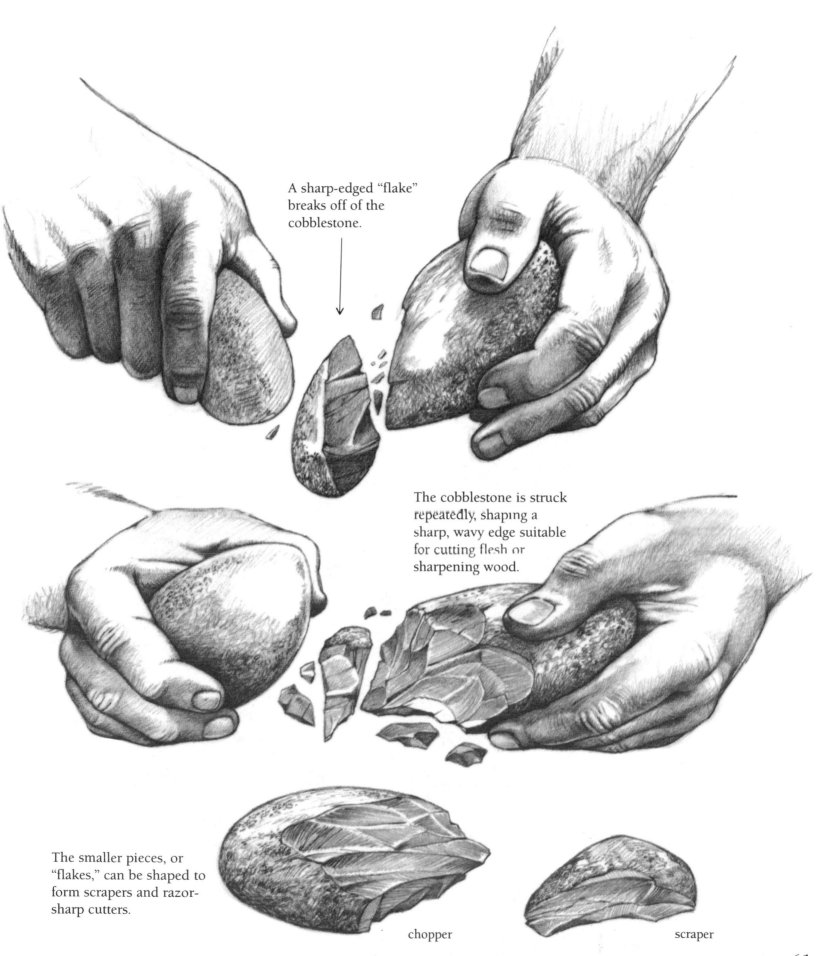

A sharp-edged "flake" breaks off of the cobblestone.

The cobblestone is struck repeatedly, shaping a sharp, wavy edge suitable for cutting flesh or sharpening wood.

The smaller pieces, or "flakes," can be shaped to form scrapers and razor-sharp cutters.

chopper

scraper

From the beginning, *Homo* species lived in close-knit bands. They could not outrun predators or defend themselves with their teeth. Their only defense was to help one another. They may have developed advanced communication which led to language, and close social relationships. This may have had something to do with making their brains grow larger. At first they did not have permanent homes but lived a nomadic life, camping at sites near their food and water sources.

Although they were eating more meat, they probably still consumed fruits, nuts, seeds, roots, tubers, and possibly insects. They apparently hunted for food in groups. We don't know for sure if they shared food, but they probably did. Later they established per-

manent home bases and discovered the use of fire. They began living in shelters. Some built their shelters; others lived in caves. These hominids were almost surely bringing food back to their home base. They still were not modern humans, but they were getting closer.

The earliest known *Homo* species lived in Africa—mostly along the edges of enormous lakes or one of the many rivers or streams that flowed into them. There they had fresh water as well as trees for shade and protection. Among the animal bones found at their campsites were those of hippopotamuses, giraffes, pigs, porcupines, waterbucks, gazelles, and wildebeests. We can't be sure that all of these were eaten by these hominids, but it seems the most likely explanation.

About 1.5 million years ago some of the *Homo* species began to leave Africa and go to Asia and Europe. Finally they colonized the rest of the world. Today they live on every continent on earth.

Homo species changed very slowly for the first two million years of their existence. About forty thousand years ago modern humans came on the scene. Since then there has been a rapid change in *Homo,* both in life-style and in appearance.

There is some argument among scientists as to how many species of *Homo* there were. Some think there were only two. Some say five or six. Most believe that there were three species: *Homo habilis,* the oldest; *Homo erectus,* the nearest to our species; and *Homo sapiens,* the species to which modern humans belong. Many scientists divide *Homo sapiens* into subspecies.

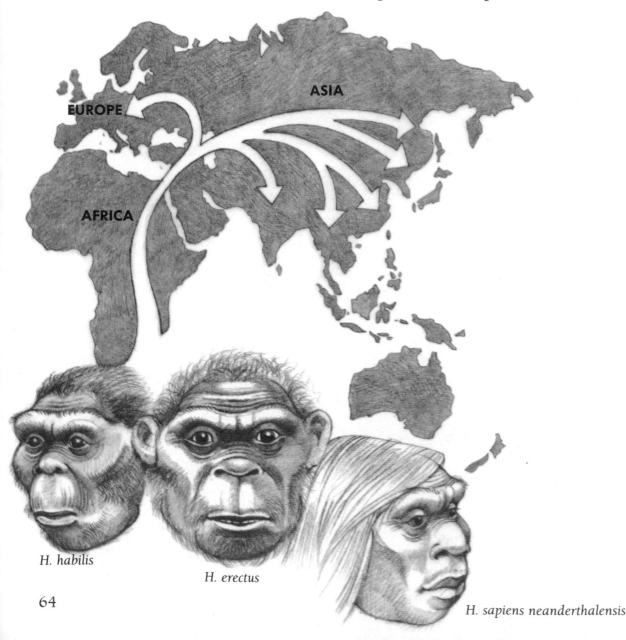

H. habilis

H. erectus

H. sapiens neanderthalensis

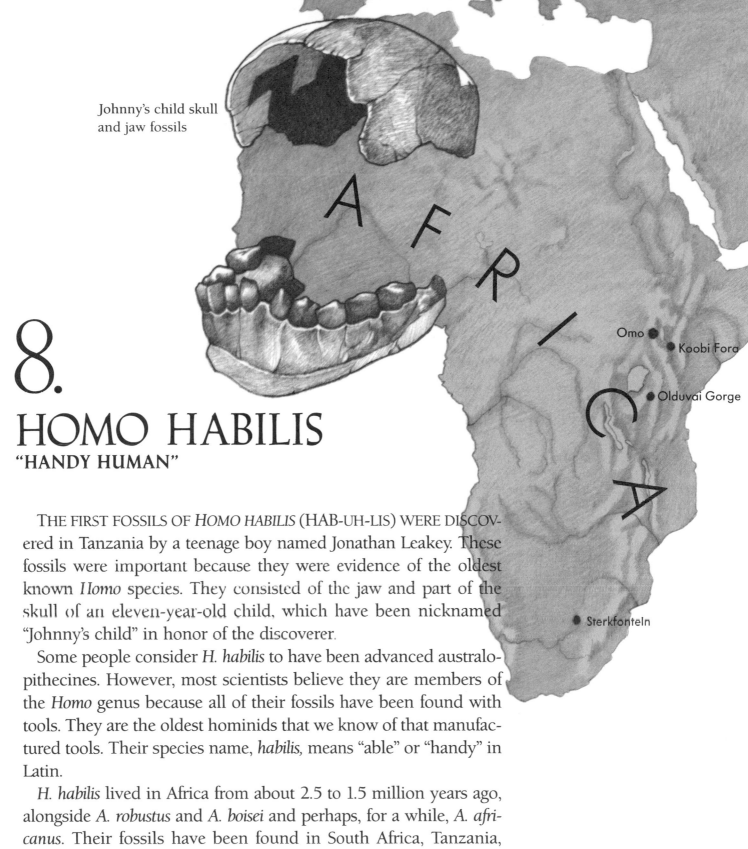

Johnny's child skull and jaw fossils

AFRICA

Omo
Koobi Fora

Olduvai Gorge

Sterkfontein

8.

HOMO HABILIS
"HANDY HUMAN"

THE FIRST FOSSILS OF *HOMO HABILIS* (HAB-UH-LIS) WERE DISCOV-
ered in Tanzania by a teenage boy named Jonathan Leakey. These
fossils were important because they were evidence of the oldest
known *Homo* species. They consisted of the jaw and part of the
skull of an eleven-year-old child, which have been nicknamed
"Johnny's child" in honor of the discoverer.

Some people consider *H. habilis* to have been advanced australopithecines. However, most scientists believe they are members of
the *Homo* genus because all of their fossils have been found with
tools. They are the oldest hominids that we know of that manufactured tools. Their species name, *habilis,* means "able" or "handy" in
Latin.

H. habilis lived in Africa from about 2.5 to 1.5 million years ago,
alongside *A. robustus* and *A. boisei* and perhaps, for a while, *A. africanus.* Their fossils have been found in South Africa, Tanzania,
Kenya, and Ethiopia. Many were found in the same deposits as the
australopithecines. Their tools have also been found in Zaire. They
probably lived all over Africa.

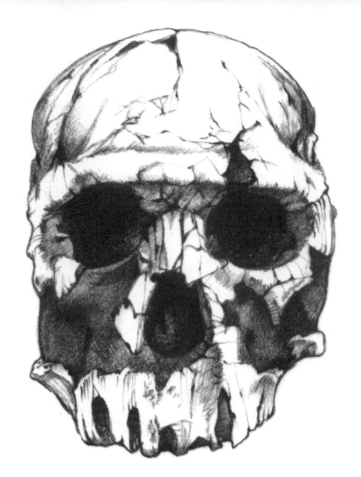

Skull 1470

Although a complete skeleton of a single individual has not yet been found, almost every part of the skeleton is represented from sixteen different individuals. These parts consist of many jaws, hundreds of teeth, arm and leg bones, feet, hands, ribs, vertebrae, a pelvis, and six skulls. They also include parts of another child—the lower jaw, bits of upper jaw, a patch of skull, and some hand bones—nicknamed "Cindy."

One of the most important *H. habilis* fossils is a nearly perfect skull known as 1470 (its catalogue number). Only the lower jaw is missing. When found, this skull was in three hundred pieces—none larger than a matchbox and most smaller than a fingernail. It took a scientist five weeks to glue the skull together. Another skull, nicknamed "Twiggy," was also nearly complete, but it had been badly flattened by the weight of the sediment above it.

A partial skull (dubbed "George") was left overnight where it had been found because it was too late in the day to dig it out. Unfortunately, a herd of cattle stampeded down the gully that night and crushed most of the skull to powder. All that was left of "George" were a few small fragments and the teeth.

Although *H. habilis* resembled the smaller australopithecines in some ways, they were more advanced physically and mentally. These short, slender, pygmy-sized hominids were three to five feet tall and weighed from 80 to 113 pounds when fully grown. Females were much smaller than males. *H. habilis*'s arms were long like those of australopithecines, but their delicate skeletal bones were more similar to those of modern humans than to those of the australopithecines. The hands and feet were almost identical to ours.

The face was somewhat flatter and less heavily browed than an australopithecine's. The skull was thinner, higher-domed, and more rounded than the skull of that hominid. Its 775-cubic-centimeter (1.5-pint) cranial capacity was greater than that of an australopithecine, but still quite small compared to ours. The shape and size of the jaws were similar to those of modern humans. The incisors and canines were a little larger than those of the australopithecines, but the molars were smaller and shaped differently. Wear on the teeth shows that they chewed both meat and plant food.

Some *H. habilis* fossils and tools were discovered in a cave in South Africa. However, it is not known whether the hominids lived in the cave or what they were doing there. Most of their fossils have been found in East Africa.

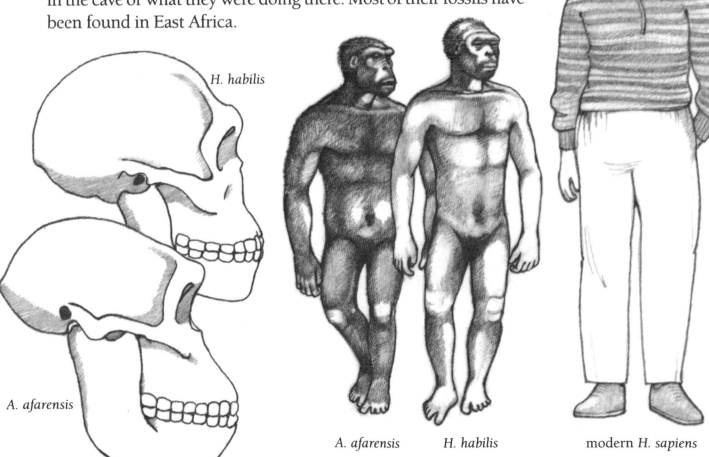

H. habilis

A. afarensis

A. afarensis   *H. habilis*   modern *H. sapiens*

wild figs

Thousands of animal bones and stone tools found in East Africa indicate that these hominids lived in open-air campsites along ancient riverbanks and on the shores of prehistoric lakes. East Africa at that time was a warm, open grassland, just as it is now. Many streams and rivers flowed into the lakes. Groups of *H. habilis*—probably members of a single family—apparently stayed in one spot for a few days or weeks, then moved on again in search of food. They camped on soft ground near fresh water where food was plentiful and trees could provide shade and a place to escape from predators.

We know from impressions of wild fig tree leaves that fruit grew in the region. *H. habilis* probably ate many kinds of fruit as well as berries, succulent shoots, tubers, greens, nuts, insects, and bird eggs. Bones found at the campsites show that they also ate catfish, frogs, tortoises, shorebirds, young pigs, young giant ostriches, rats, mice, lizards, and snakes.

The earliest evidence of manufactured tools is provided by two tools made from antelope antlers and bones, which were found in the South African cave. They may have been digging tools.

H. habilis may have started making stone tools in order to cut meat from large animals. Their tools were very simple, requiring only the ability to break a sharp fragment from a stone by hitting it in a certain way with a small river pebble.

The East African tools were made of volcanic rock (basalt and chert), which was the best kind of rock available because it fractures easily. This kind of stone was not always available near the *H. habilis* campsites. Sometimes it was necessary for the hominids to walk as far as nine miles to find places where the rock occurred naturally.

Generally they made tools from oblong, rounded cobbles—some as big as a croquet ball, others as small as a golf ball. A sharp edge was formed by chipping flakes off one side. Their tool kit (which scientists call the Oldowan tool kit, because these tools were first found in Olduvai Gorge) consisted of choppers, scrapers, and blades (or knives). These tools were extremely sharp and apparently were used only for butchering and scraping.

Cut marks left on animal bone by sharp-edged cutting stones used to butcher the animal

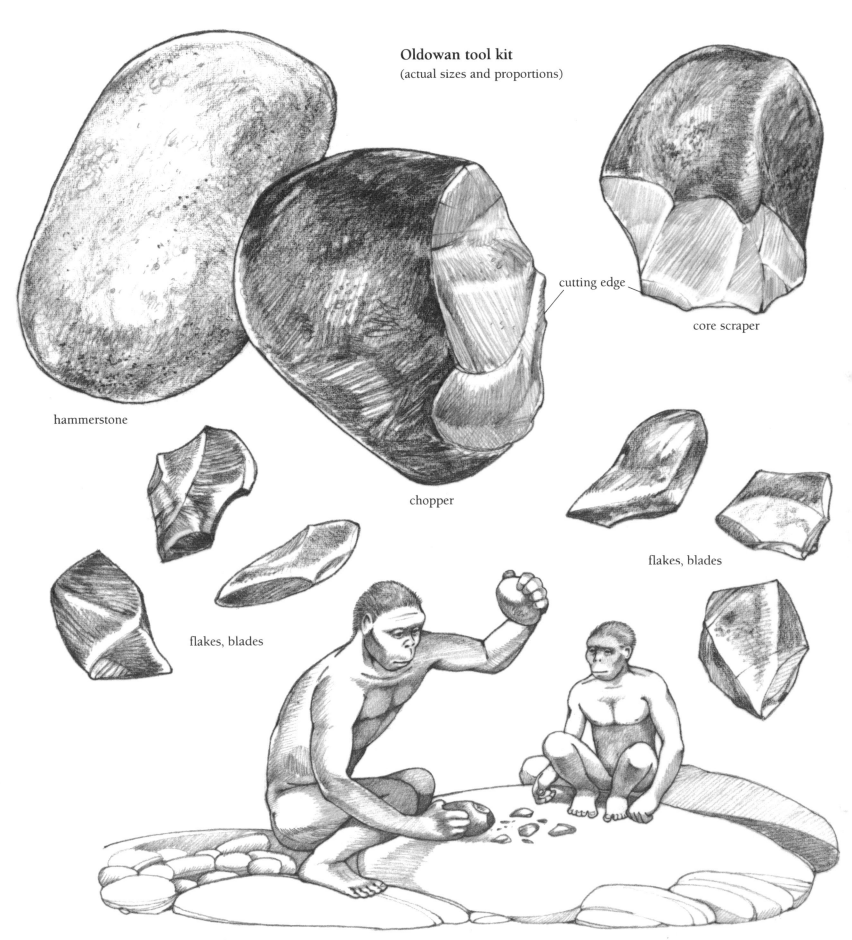

Oldowan tool kit
(actual sizes and proportions)

cutting edge

core scraper

hammerstone

chopper

flakes, blades

flakes, blades

flakes, blades

Bones found at campsites indicate that leg bones from large animals such as elephants and rhinos—twice as large as a modern East African black rhino—were sometimes cut off at the joint and taken back to camp. Perhaps this food was shared with mates and young. Parts of many different animals have been found at campsites. It is not known whether the toolmakers killed these animals. They certainly butchered them. Marks on the bones clearly show that they had been cut or scraped by stone tools.

H. habilis probably could not have killed a large rhino or an elephant. They may have butchered weakened or already dead animals. Or they may have scavenged meat by frightening a lion, saber-toothed tiger, or other predator from its fresh kill. Some of the cut marks on the bones were on top of tooth marks made by a predator. This clearly shows that the hominids got to the meat after the predator.

These hominids may have used a combined bully and sneak strategy to drive off a predator. This would have been dangerous, and most likely possible only if they worked together in large groups. Dying or weakened animals could have been found easily by watching for vultures circling in the sky. On a savanna, there is almost always a fresh kill available somewhere.

71

Sometimes *H. habilis* made tools and ate the meat on the spot where a large animal was butchered. At other campsites there is no evidence of meat having been eaten at all, even though there are a great number of stone chips indicating that many stone tools had been made there. Scientists believe these sites may have been tool factories.

There is no evidence that *H. habilis* cooked their meat or used fire in any way. There is evidence that they stripped tendons and hides from the carcasses. We have no way of knowing what they did with the tendons and hides, but perhaps they made the hides into bags to carry food in.

These resourceful hominids lived side by side with the australopithecines for about a million years. Then around 1.6 million years ago a larger-brained *Homo* species, *Homo erectus,* appeared on the scene. Shortly afterward *Homo habilis* disappeared from the fossil record. They were replaced by the larger-brained hominid.

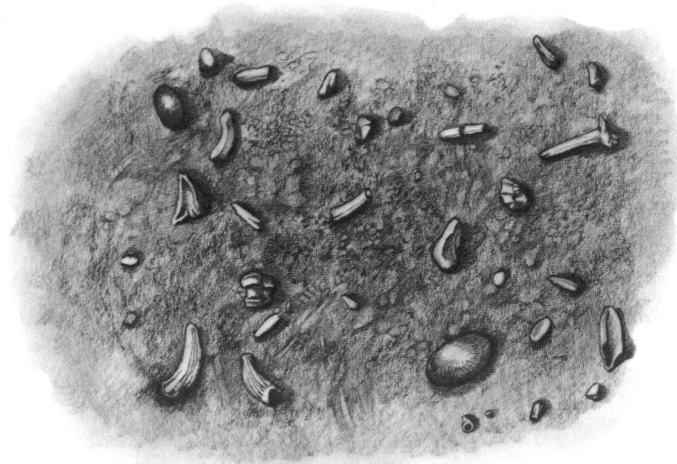

Stone and bone fossil remains at a habiline camp at
Olduvai Gorge, Tanzania

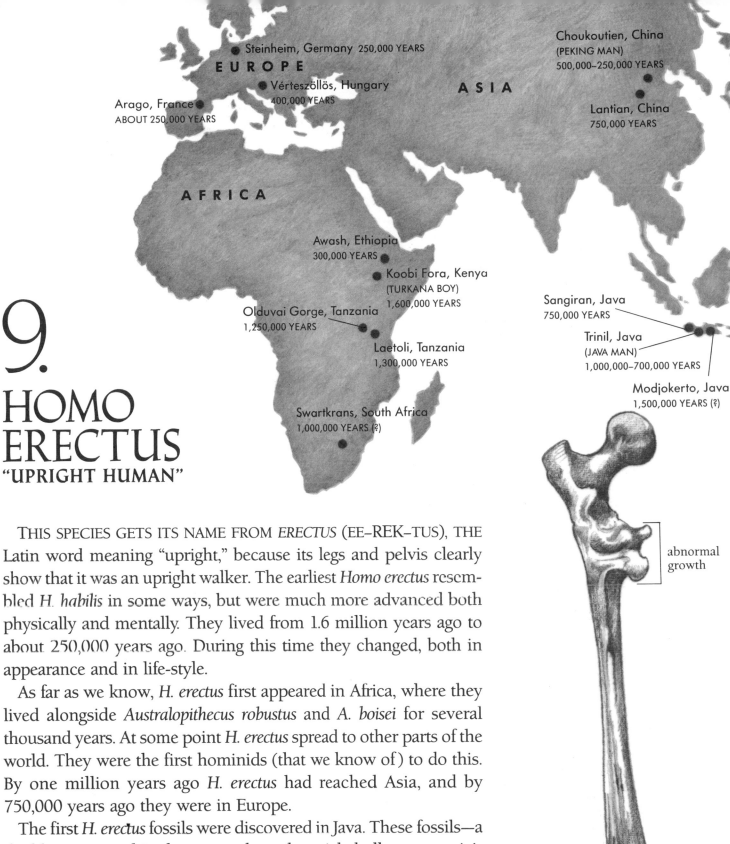

Steinheim, Germany 250,000 YEARS

E U R O P E

Vérteszöllös, Hungary
400,000 YEARS

A S I A

Choukoutien, China
(PEKING MAN)
500,000–250,000 YEARS

Arago, France
ABOUT 250,000 YEARS

Lantian, China
750,000 YEARS

A F R I C A

Awash, Ethiopia
300,000 YEARS

Koobi Fora, Kenya
(TURKANA BOY)
1,600,000 YEARS

Sangiran, Java
750,000 YEARS

Olduvai Gorge, Tanzania
1,250,000 YEARS

Trinil, Java
(JAVA MAN)
1,000,000–700,000 YEARS

Laetoli, Tanzania
1,300,000 YEARS

Modjokerto, Java
1,500,000 YEARS (?)

Swartkrans, South Africa
1,000,000 YEARS (?)

9.
HOMO ERECTUS
"UPRIGHT HUMAN"

THIS SPECIES GETS ITS NAME FROM *ERECTUS* (EE–REK–TUS), THE Latin word meaning "upright," because its legs and pelvis clearly show that it was an upright walker. The earliest *Homo erectus* resembled *H. habilis* in some ways, but were much more advanced both physically and mentally. They lived from 1.6 million years ago to about 250,000 years ago. During this time they changed, both in appearance and in life-style.

As far as we know, *H. erectus* first appeared in Africa, where they lived alongside *Australopithecus robustus* and *A. boisei* for several thousand years. At some point *H. erectus* spread to other parts of the world. They were the first hominids (that we know of) to do this. By one million years ago *H. erectus* had reached Asia, and by 750,000 years ago they were in Europe.

The first *H. erectus* fossils were discovered in Java. These fossils—a thighbone, several jawbones, teeth, and partial skulls—were originally named *Pithecanthropus* (PITH-ee-kan-THROP-us) *erectus*, but are better known as Java Man.

abnormal growth

thighbone fossil from Trinil, Java

73

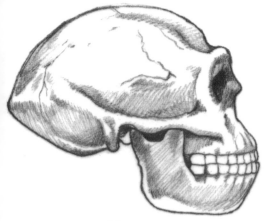

Peking Man skull

side view

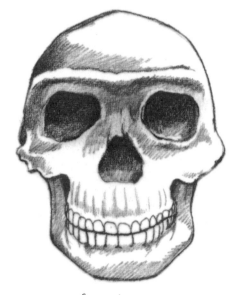

front view

Hundreds of similar fossils were later discovered in Asia and northeastern Africa. It became evident that this hominid belonged in the same genus as modern humans, so the name was changed to *Homo erectus*.

Some of the most famous *H. erectus* fossils were found in a cave near Peking, China. These 750,000-year-old fossils—the partial remains of forty individuals—were originally named *Sinanthropus pekinensis* (sin-an-THROP-us pee-kin-EN-sis) but are commonly called Peking Man. Peking Man had occupied the cave for 230,000 years. They left behind twenty thousand tools and other artifacts, which provide valuable clues about the lives of these hominids.

The African *H. erectus* fossils are much older and more complete than those found in Asia. They include two partial skeletons. Unfortunately the first, a female, had suffered from a severe bone disease. Her 1.5-million-year-old fossils (part of the skull, the lower jaw, some vertebrae, ribs, leg bones, and much of the pelvis) are too distorted by the disease to be useful in determining the appearance of *H. erectus*.

The second, however, is in perfect condition, and is the most complete skeleton of an early hominid found so far. Only the left arm, the lower right arm, and the hands and feet are missing. This skeleton, of a twelve-year-old boy, was discovered in Kenya near Lake Turkana. It is one of the most important hominid discoveries ever made. The Turkana boy is 1.6 million years old—the oldest known *H. erectus*. It shows, for the first time, how large these hominids were and what they looked like.

H. erectus were much taller than anyone had suspected. At age twelve the Turkana boy was already bigger than *H. habilis*. He was about five feet four inches tall and may have weighed 140 pounds. If he had lived to be an adult, he might have grown to be six feet tall. He was stockily built, and his heavy bones suggest that he was much stronger than modern humans. His skeleton was almost identical to that of a modern boy, but his skull was different.

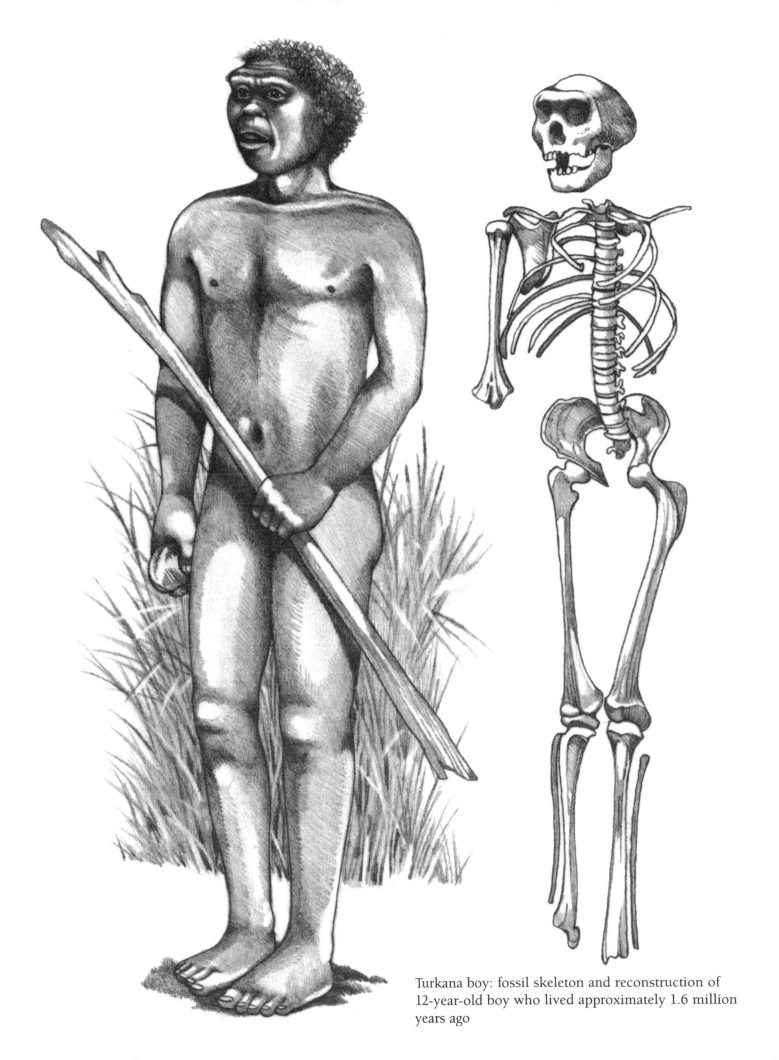

Turkana boy: fossil skeleton and reconstruction of
12-year-old boy who lived approximately 1.6 million
years ago

75

More than twenty partial *H. erectus* skulls have been found, but only the skull of the Turkana boy shows what the face may have looked like. The face was small, and, as in *H. habilis*, the skull bones were thick; the forehead was short and sloping. Heavy brow ridges jutted out over the eyes. Unlike *H. habilis, H. erectus* had a small but poorly developed chin and smaller teeth, more like those of a modern human. Although the jaws were long with strong muscles, they protruded less than those of *H. habilis*.

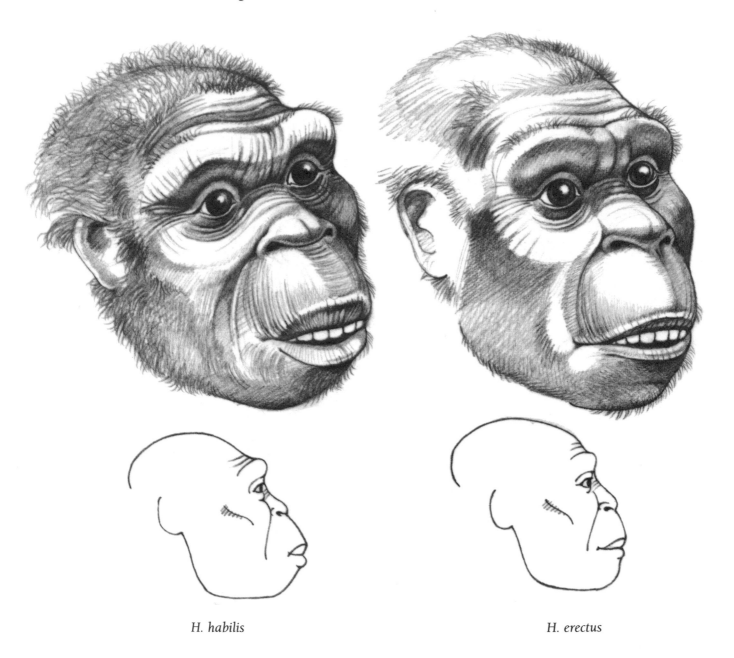

H. habilis   H. erectus

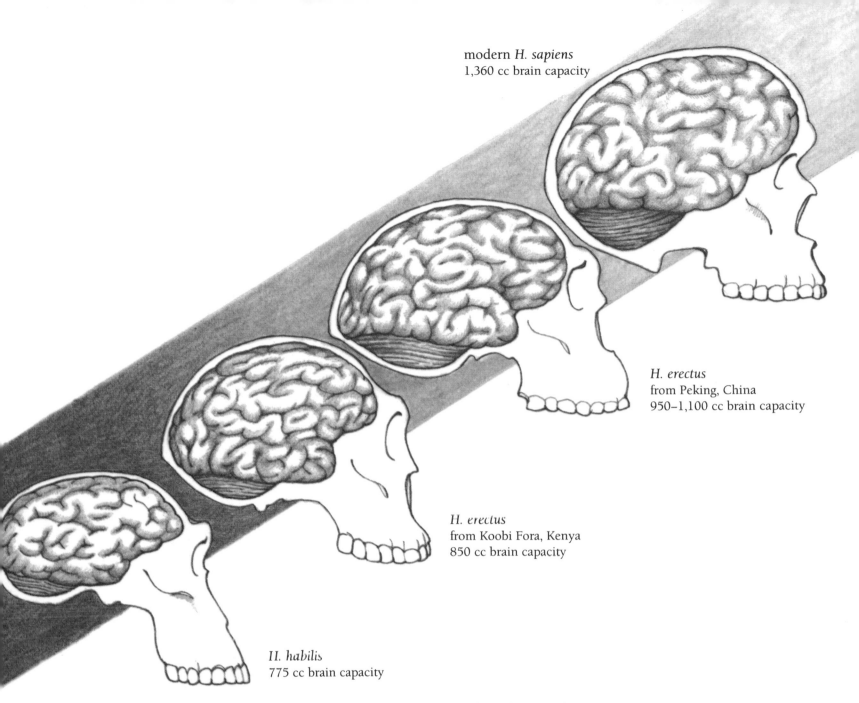

modern *H. sapiens*
1,360 cc brain capacity

H. erectus
from Peking, China
950–1,100 cc brain capacity

H. erectus
from Koobi Fora, Kenya
850 cc brain capacity

H. habilis
775 cc brain capacity

The greatest difference, however, was in the size of the brain. The grapefruit-sized brain (about 850 cubic centimeters) of the earliest *H. erectus* was considerably larger and more complex than that of *H. habilis*. Asian specimens had even larger brains—950 cubic centimeters. Cranial capacities of the latest known *H. erectus* reached 1,200 cubic centimeters (well over two pints, about 75 percent of that of a modern human). As the brain grew, the cranium expanded, and the jaw and tooth size shrank. The skull became thinner and the brow ridges smaller. The life-styles of later *H. erectus* became more sophisticated.

H. erectus lived in a variety of environments, from tropical savannas and open woodlands in Africa to temperate woodlands and forest tundra in Europe and Asia. They were the first hominids to live in temperate climates and were apparently widespread in Europe as well as Africa and Asia. Although only a few fossils have been found in Europe, we have ample evidence of their presence there. *H. erectus* living sites have been found in Germany, Hungary, Czechoslovakia, Spain, and France.

H. erectus seem to have occupied campsites for longer periods than did *H. habilis*. In warm weather they apparently camped in lightly wooded places near streams or on sandy beaches along the shores of lakes or seas. Groups of from four to thirty may have lived together at a single site for three or four months at a time. Sometimes they returned to the same place year after year.

Many built rough shelters. Remains of 400,000-year-old oval-shaped structures have been found in France. These were forty feet long and twenty feet wide. The walls were made of young branches supported in the center by a row of sturdy posts. Large stones circled the base of the walls. Each hut had a hearth or firepit in the floor.

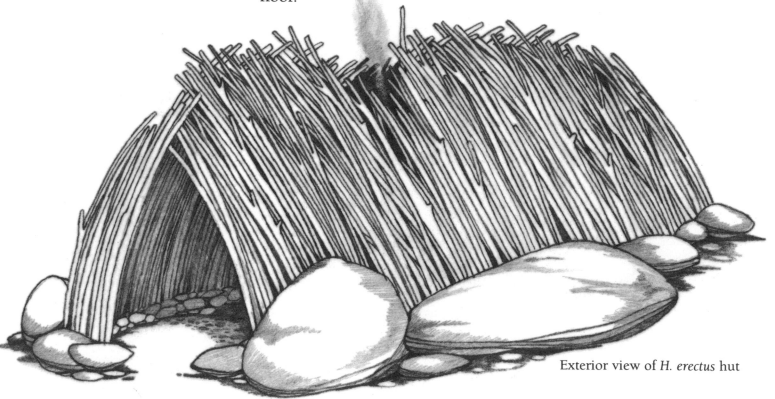

Exterior view of *H. erectus* hut

RIGHT: Interior of *H. erectus* hut with hearth in the floor and chimney opening above, 400,000 years ago

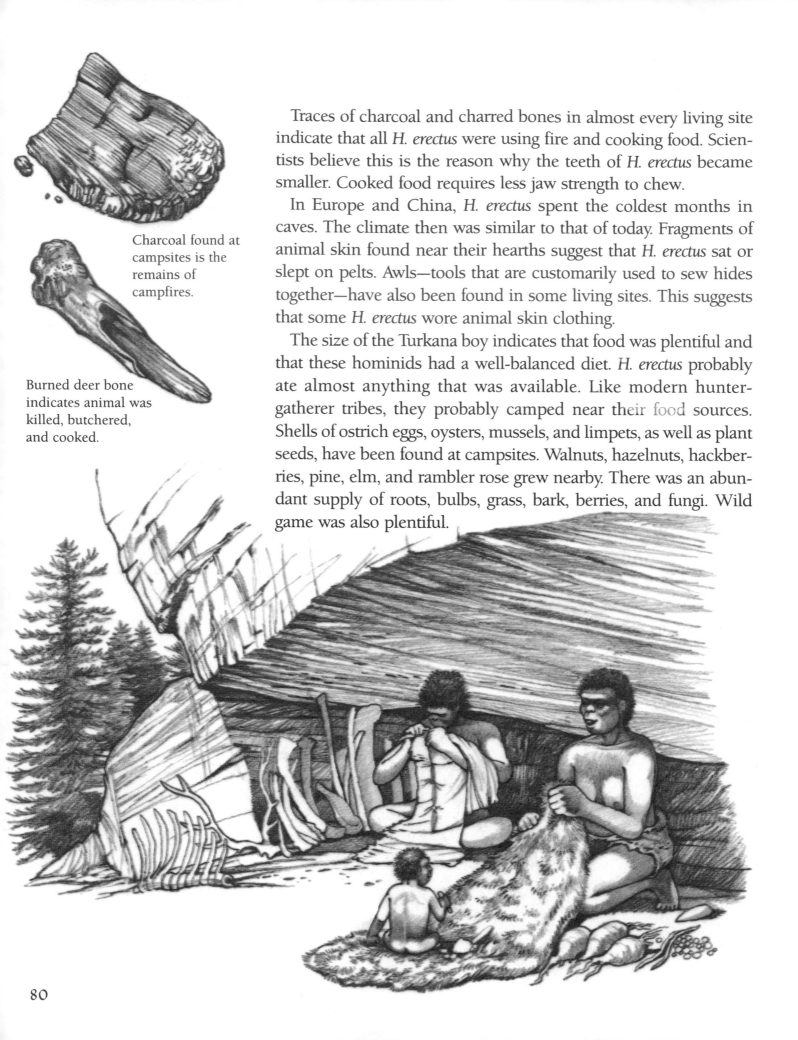

Charcoal found at campsites is the remains of campfires.

Burned deer bone indicates animal was killed, butchered, and cooked.

Traces of charcoal and charred bones in almost every living site indicate that all *H. erectus* were using fire and cooking food. Scientists believe this is the reason why the teeth of *H. erectus* became smaller. Cooked food requires less jaw strength to chew.

In Europe and China, *H. erectus* spent the coldest months in caves. The climate then was similar to that of today. Fragments of animal skin found near their hearths suggest that *H. erectus* sat or slept on pelts. Awls—tools that are customarily used to sew hides together—have also been found in some living sites. This suggests that some *H. erectus* wore animal skin clothing.

The size of the Turkana boy indicates that food was plentiful and that these hominids had a well-balanced diet. *H. erectus* probably ate almost anything that was available. Like modern hunter-gatherer tribes, they probably camped near their food sources. Shells of ostrich eggs, oysters, mussels, and limpets, as well as plant seeds, have been found at campsites. Walnuts, hazelnuts, hackberries, pine, elm, and rambler rose grew nearby. There was an abundant supply of roots, bulbs, grass, bark, berries, and fungi. Wild game was also plentiful.

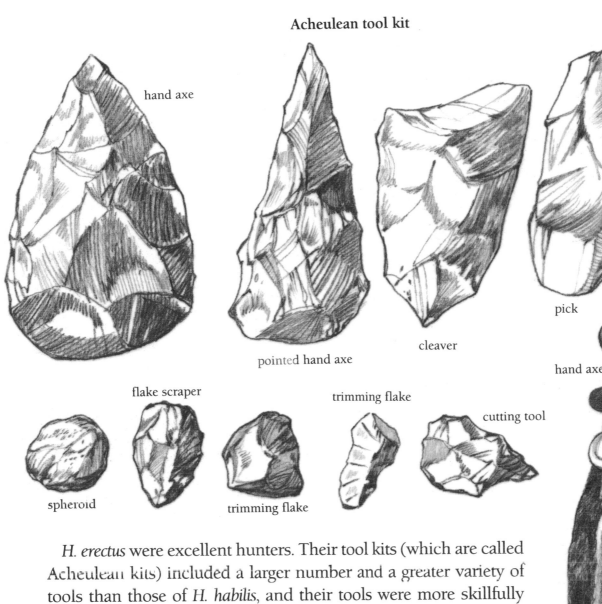

hand axe

pointed hand axe

cleaver

pick

hand axe

flake scraper

trimming flake

cutting tool

spheroid

trimming flake

H. erectus were excellent hunters. Their tool kits (which are called Acheulean kits) included a larger number and a greater variety of tools than those of *H. habilis*, and their tools were more skillfully made. They were smaller, sharper, better patterned, and made of harder materials. They included anvils, choppers, chisels, hammerstones, cleavers, picks, scrapers, punches, and awls. Scientists have found rounded stones that some think may have been fastened together with strips of animal skin. These could have been used as bolas, to entangle the legs of animals. Others suggest that the stones were thrown like baseballs at prey.

One of *H. erectus*'s best-known inventions was the hand axe—an almond-shaped tool with two sharp edges, five inches to a foot or more in length. Some think the hand axe was thrown like a discus and was probably used to kill prey. The axes have mostly been found near streams or watering holes.

H. erectus hunted elephants, rhinos, mountain goats, giant boars, wild oxen, giant sheep, antlered giraffes, wild asses, deer, and warthogs. Most were young animals. The favorite meat seems to have been deer. Most of these animals were both faster and larger than the hominids.

Hunting of large and swift animals is difficult and dangerous. A successful hunt requires several participants plus organization and planning. The fact that *H. erectus* killed many large animals suggests that these hominids could communicate well with one another. As their brain capacities increased, so did their hunting skills. They were able to devise complicated strategies to catch their prey. Sometimes they banded together to drive huge animals into bogs, where they killed and butchered them. Evidence found in Spain suggests that some used rings of fire to drive elephants into a marsh. Apparently the meat was then taken back to the cave and shared with mates and children.

Improved hunting skills gave *H. erectus* more time for other activities and they began to practice rituals. Some laid bones of large animals in curious patterns. For example, at one site in Spain, elephant bones had been placed in a "T" formation. No one knows the reason for this, but scientists believe that it is evidence of some kind of religious ceremony. This belief is strengthened by the discovery at the site of traces of ochre, a mineral used for body paint.

Homo erectus was a very successful species for more than a million years. For half a million years, they were the only hominids in existence. They were intelligent, adaptable, and caring individuals. They used fire, hunted big game, built shelters, developed culture, and perhaps had a religion of sorts, and they spread to many parts of the world. Most scientists believe these hominids were the direct ancestors of *Homo sapiens* (SAY-pee-enz). The latest ones, those from 300,000 to 250,000 years ago, looked so much like the earliest *H. sapiens*, who appeared about 250,000 years ago, that some class them as *H. sapiens*. However, their tool kit was the same as that of *H. erectus* and therefore most scientists consider them advanced *H. erectus*.

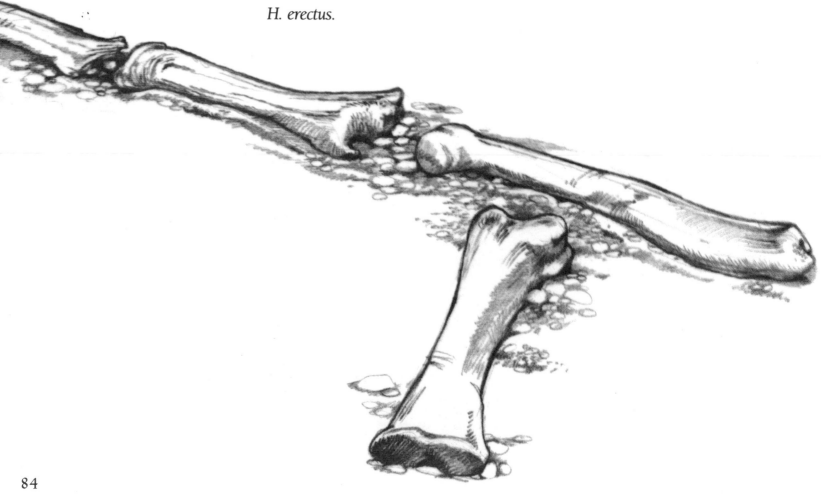

archaic *Homo sapiens*

Homo sapiens neanderthalensis

Homo sapiens sapiens (modern)

10.
HOMO SAPIENS
"WISE PERSON"

HOMO SAPIENS IS THE SCIENTIFIC NAME FOR HUMAN BEINGS. THE name means "wise person" in Latin. Our species was given this name because its members have the largest brains of all the hominids and are assumed to be the most intelligent. Certainly they have made greater cultural and technological advances than any other hominid species.

This species is divided into three subspecies: archaic *Homo sapiens, Homo sapiens neanderthalensis* (nee-AN-der-tal-EN-sis), and *Homo sapiens sapiens* (the subspecies to which modern humans belong).

Little is known about the earliest or archaic *Homo sapiens,* but we have evidence that they were widespread in Europe, Asia, and Africa. No one knows for sure when they first appeared. Most scientists think that it was about 250,000 years ago. There is little agreement on where this happened. Some think it was in Europe; some claim it was in eastern or central Asia; others are sure it was in Africa. Still others suggest that perhaps *Homo sapiens* appeared in all four places at about the same time. We won't know the answer to this riddle until many more fossils have been found.

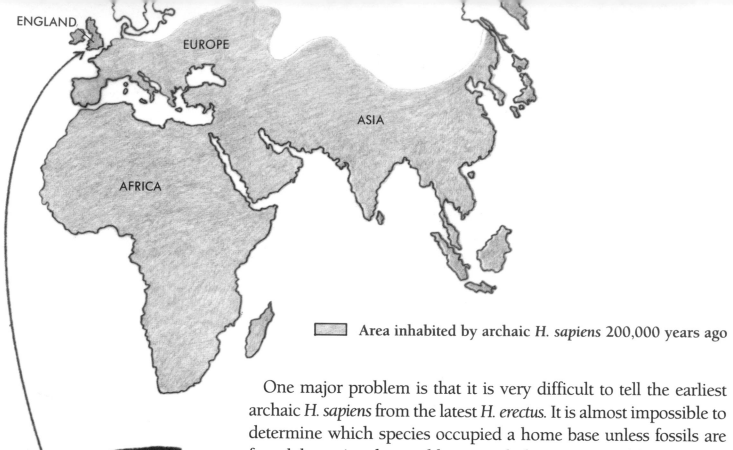

Area inhabited by archaic *H. sapiens* 200,000 years ago

Rear skull fossil pieces from Swanscombe, England, the first archaic *H. sapiens* fossil discovered

One major problem is that it is very difficult to tell the earliest archaic *H. sapiens* from the latest *H. erectus*. It is almost impossible to determine which species occupied a home base unless fossils are found there. Another problem is with dating. Many of the sites cannot be accurately dated, and therefore there is no way of knowing how or when they fit into the entire picture.

Very few fossils of archaic *H. sapiens* have been found so far. Those that have been found are fragmentary. Fortunately, some exceptionally good skulls are among those few.

The oldest fossils that can be identified positively as *H. sapiens* were found in Europe. One, a nearly complete skull of a twenty-year-old woman, is the oldest *H. sapiens* fossil known. It and another skull were found in Germany.

The first archaic *H. sapiens* fossil discovered was found in England, not far from London. It was the back part of a female's skull. She, too, had been about twenty years old when she died. Thousands of stone tools, very similar to those of *H. erectus,* were found with the 200,000-year-old skull. We know, however, that she was *H. sapiens* rather than *H. erectus* because her skull was shaped more like that of a modern human than like that of *H. erectus.*

A similar 200,000-year-old skull and two jaws were found in France. Other archaic *H. sapiens* fossils are known from Greece, Italy, and Yugoslavia.

86

Later fossil remains—craniums, jaws, several teeth, and other bone fragments—have been found in Africa and Asia. These date from 100,000 to 40,000 years ago. The oldest were somewhat more primitive than the most recent.

The very earliest *H. sapiens* were about halfway between *H. erectus* and modern humans in appearance. Their skeletons were almost identical to ours, since even those of *H. erectus* were quite modern, but there were some differences in the skull.

The cranium was low and thick, the nose was broad, and the forehead was short, similar to those of *H. erectus*. However, in other ways the head of archaic *H. sapiens* was quite unlike that of *H. erectus*. Although the brows were large and heavy, they were less massive than those of the earlier hominids. The braincase was larger. Its capacity was between 1,100 and 1,450 cubic centimeters (more than three pints). As their brains grew, the forehead region bulged more, and the brow ridges became less distinct. The back of the braincase was rounded, more like a modern human's, instead of sloping like that of *H. erectus*. The jaws were also very similar in shape to those of modern humans. Although the front teeth were large, the molars were quite modern. The vocal tract was fully modern. Archaic *H. sapiens* may have been capable of talking as well as we do, but probably did not.

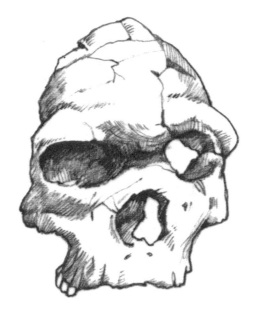

Skull fossil of *H. sapiens* from cave of Arago at Toutavel, France, approximately 200,000 years old

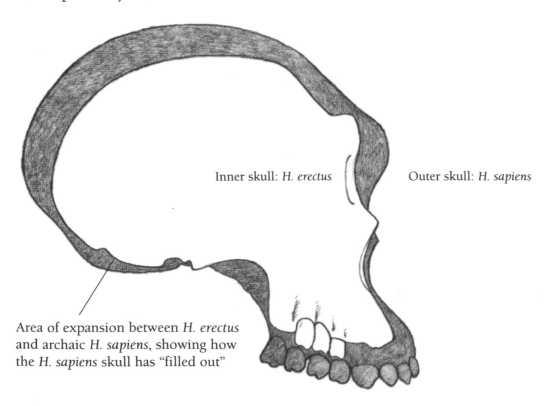

Inner skull: *H. erectus*

Outer skull: *H. sapiens*

Area of expansion between *H. erectus* and archaic *H. sapiens*, showing how the *H. sapiens* skull has "filled out"

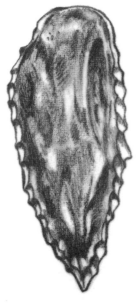

teardrop hand axe

The life-style of these early *H. sapiens* was probably very much like that of *H. erectus*. Their stone tools, though similar to those of *H. erectus*, were somewhat better made. Their oldest tool kits were found in Europe and consisted of beautifully notched and saw-toothed utensils made of flint that had been worked on both sides. Scrapers for cleaning hides; knives for butchering, woodworking, slicing, or cutting plant material; engravers for decorating bone or antlers; and teardrop-shaped hand axes have been found. In other parts of the Old World these same kinds of tools were made of basalt, quartzite or quartz, and obsidian (volcanic glass).

These people used advanced techniques to work their materials. For example, antlers, which are too hard to be cut when dry, were soaked in water until soft enough to cut. Archaic *H. sapiens* also invented tools for boring holes in wood and bone. These boring tools were turned clockwise, which suggests that these early *H. sapiens* tended to be right-handed.

Like *H. erectus*, some archaic *H. sapiens* lived in caves, others in open country. Their open-country shelters were constructed of branches and animal hides. Apparently, two or more families lived together. Fire was used to cook food. They probably knew how to start their own fires.

The climate of Europe 200,000 years ago was mild—much warmer than it is now. This was a period between two ice ages. Plant food and wild game were plentiful. Elephants, rhinoceroses, wild boar, deer, giant oxen, musk oxen, cave bears, horses, lions, panthers, beavers, and many kinds of rodents roamed the open grasslands.

Sometime around 150,000 years ago, the climate turned cold as ice started to creep down from the Scandinavian mountains and a new ice age began. The ice sheet covered most of England and northern Europe.

It was during this period that a new group of *Homo sapiens*, the subspecies *Homo sapiens neanderthalensis*, appeared in Europe. This subspecies completely replaced archaic *Homo sapiens* in Europe, although they continued to flourish in Asia and Africa.

archaic *H. sapiens*

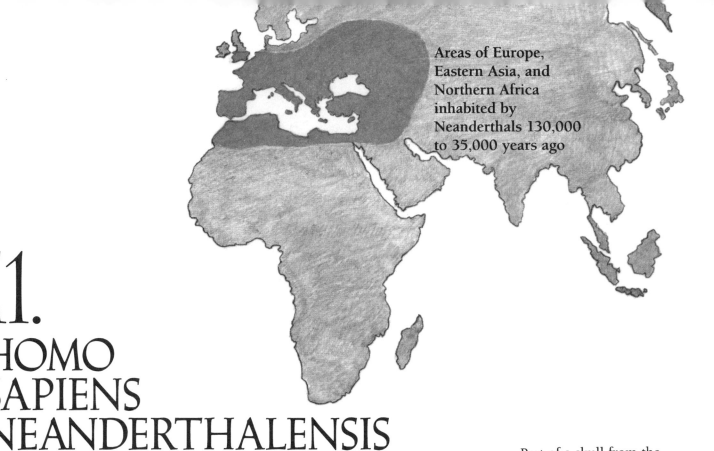

Areas of Europe, Eastern Asia, and Northern Africa inhabited by Neanderthals 130,000 to 35,000 years ago

11.
HOMO SAPIENS NEANDERTHALENSIS
"WISE PERSON FROM NEANDER VALLEY"

THE FIRST EXTINCT HOMINID EVER FOUND WAS A MEMBER OF THE subspecies *Homo sapiens neanderthalensis*. This subspecies is also the best known of the extinct hominids and perhaps the most argued about. For a long time these hominids were believed to be a separate species from *Homo sapiens* and were called *H. neanderthalensis*. Only after much more evidence was found was it recognized that these people were *H. sapiens*. They were more primitive than modern humans, but they had a more advanced technology and a more sophisticated social life than archaic *H. sapiens* or *Homo erectus*.

The name *neanderthalensis* comes from Neander, the name of the valley in Germany where the first specimen to be described was found. *Thal* (pronounced TAL) is the German word for "valley." These hominids are usually called Neanderthals for short.

The oldest known Neanderthal fossils were found in Egypt in deposits 130,000 years old. The most recent are about 35,000 years old. Neanderthal remains have been found in several places in Africa and Asia and in almost every country of Europe.

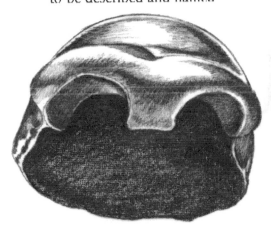

Part of a skull from the Neander Valley, Germany, the first Neanderthal fossil to be described and named

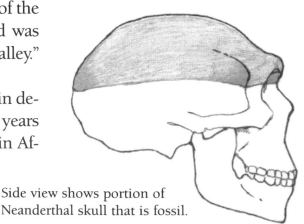

Side view shows portion of Neanderthal skull that is fossil.

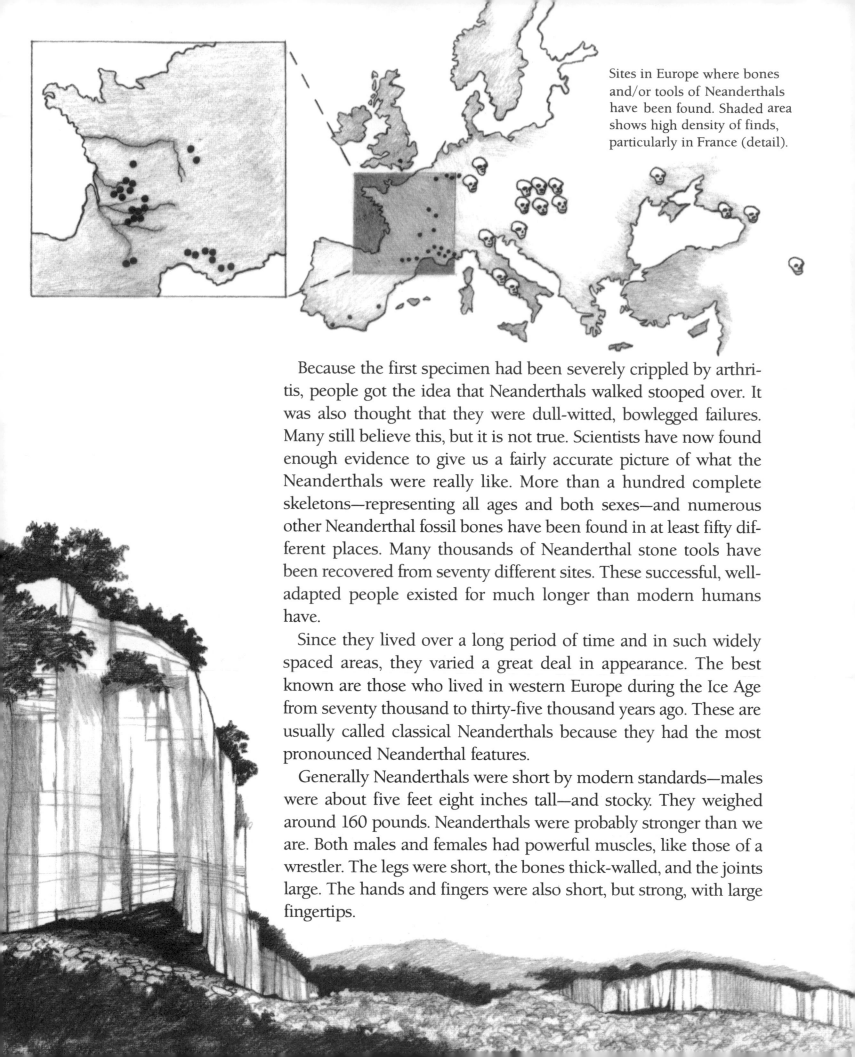

Sites in Europe where bones and/or tools of Neanderthals have been found. Shaded area shows high density of finds, particularly in France (detail).

Because the first specimen had been severely crippled by arthritis, people got the idea that Neanderthals walked stooped over. It was also thought that they were dull-witted, bowlegged failures. Many still believe this, but it is not true. Scientists have now found enough evidence to give us a fairly accurate picture of what the Neanderthals were really like. More than a hundred complete skeletons—representing all ages and both sexes—and numerous other Neanderthal fossil bones have been found in at least fifty different places. Many thousands of Neanderthal stone tools have been recovered from seventy different sites. These successful, well-adapted people existed for much longer than modern humans have.

Since they lived over a long period of time and in such widely spaced areas, they varied a great deal in appearance. The best known are those who lived in western Europe during the Ice Age from seventy thousand to thirty-five thousand years ago. These are usually called classical Neanderthals because they had the most pronounced Neanderthal features.

Generally Neanderthals were short by modern standards—males were about five feet eight inches tall—and stocky. They weighed around 160 pounds. Neanderthals were probably stronger than we are. Both males and females had powerful muscles, like those of a wrestler. The legs were short, the bones thick-walled, and the joints large. The hands and fingers were also short, but strong, with large fingertips.

Neanderthal skull and reconstructions: head and full-figure male and female

The skull, however, was shaped differently from those of other *H. sapiens*. It was rather flat on top but was long from front to back and had a distinct bulge, sometimes called a "bun," at the back. The brain was much larger than that of *Homo erectus*. Their average cranial capacity was about 1,450 cubic centimeters (a little over three pints)—the average for modern humans is 1,360 cubic centimeters. The brow ridges were heavy but smaller than those of *H. erectus*. The nose was large; the forehead sloped and the chin receded.

Neanderthal jaws are distinctive. They were large and were attached to large cheekbones with heavy muscles. The front teeth were big and had big roots. The back teeth were small and frequently had extra cusps (points on the chewing surface).

Scientists believe that Neanderthals' more distinctive features were adaptations to the cold climate. The western European Nean-

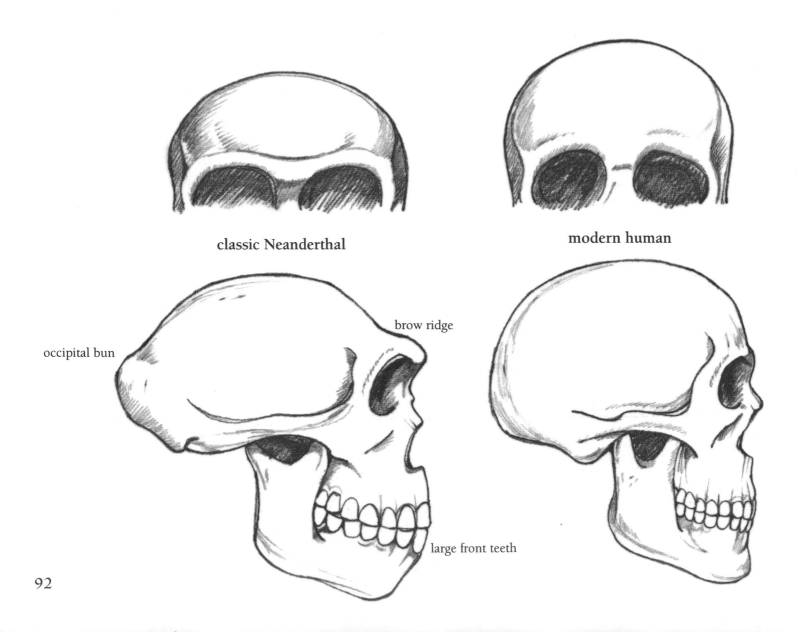

classic Neanderthal

modern human

brow ridge

occipital bun

large front teeth

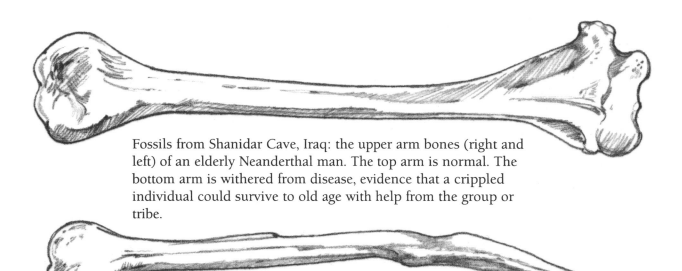

Fossils from Shanidar Cave, Iraq: the upper arm bones (right and left) of an elderly Neanderthal man. The top arm is normal. The bottom arm is withered from disease, evidence that a crippled individual could survive to old age with help from the group or tribe.

derthals were isolated from others by the glaciers that covered Europe at that time. Therefore, these characteristics became more pronounced in them.

Except for the pelvis, which was long and flattened in contrast to the short and stout pelvis of modern humans, the body of a Neanderthal was almost identical to that of a modern human. Although some were crippled by arthritis and rickets (a disease that causes bones to soften), most stood as straight and walked as well as modern humans. Given a bath and modern clothes, even a classical Neanderthal would probably not be noticed if met face to face on the street of any large city in the world today.

The earliest Neanderthals (from 130,000 to 70,000 years ago) resembled the archaic *Homo sapiens* more than they did modern humans, while the latest ones in Southwest Asia and Africa closely resembled modern humans. These Neanderthals had contact with one another and progressed toward modern humans in appearance at a fairly regular rate. By fifty thousand years ago they still had typical Neanderthal jaws, heavy brow ridges, and sloping foreheads, but their chins and skulls were more modern in shape, and the "bun" was gone.

Unlike these hominids' appearance, Neanderthals' tools varied little over the 100,000 years that they were manufactured and used, although the later ones were somewhat smaller. Neanderthals in one location made the same kind of tools as those in every other place, no matter how far apart in time or space.

Neanderthal tools were skillfully made. They were much finer and more precise than any that had come before them. Their tool kit (which scientists call the Mousterian kit) consisted of at least sixty different kinds of tools. Hunting tools were sometimes found hundreds of miles away from the source of the stone they were made from. Hide-cleaning and food-processing tools were made of flakes struck from flint or whatever other kind of stone was available locally. The flakes were delicately shaped by chipping away tiny pieces from one or more edges. Some were notched to make saw-toothed edges. Such skillful trimming required fine control of the hands and a clear idea of the desired tool.

Mousterian tool kit

Mousterian point
(actual size)

hand axe

notched tool

notched tool

These skillful craftsmen invented the stone knife, a long flint blade with one side blunt and the other sharp. They also made spear points and fine tools from bone which were used to catch fish and birds. The most common tools found at campsites were those used to scrape hides or process food.

The climate varied greatly during Neanderthals' existence, and they lived in a wide range of environments. Food was obtained by hunting, fishing, and gathering plants. Prey and plant food varied according to the region and climate. Neanderthals were skillful hunters, but gathering may have been more important in obtaining food than hunting.

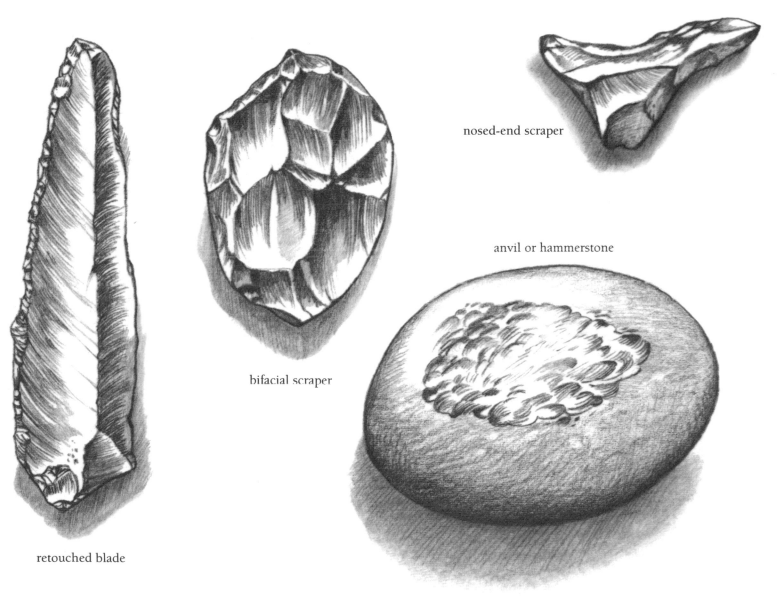

nosed-end scraper

anvil or hammerstone

bifacial scraper

retouched blade

Most Neanderthals lived in small groups of thirty-five to forty people. They did not build permanent homes, because they moved about from season to season to make the fullest use of their resources. In good weather or in warm climates they lived in open-air encampments along the shores of lakes or rivers. Sometimes their camps were occupied for many months at a time, and some were reoccupied year after year. Remains of a number of hutlike structures have been found in several places. Apparently, these had been built of branches and were probably covered with skins.

There is evidence that a large band of Neanderthals lived in one area of what is now the Nubian Desert in Egypt for 100,000 years. At that time, this area was a fairly warm, luxuriant savanna with two large lakes. The campsites were surrounded by rich vegetation and many game animals. White rhinoceroses; large buffalo, now extinct; giant camels, gazelles, antelopes, wild asses, ostriches, warthogs, jackals, small foxes, turtles, and birds were common.

Periodically the area suffered from severe drought. When this happened some of the people moved to other regions—perhaps to Europe. Until seventy thousand years ago the climate of Europe was quite similar to what it is now. The ocean level was much lower than it is today. England and Ireland were a part of the European continent. In Europe, lions, hyenas, and elephants lived alongside many of the same kinds of animals that live there today.

Then the climate changed, and huge sheets of ice covered Northern Europe and Asia. The winters were very cold, lasting four or five months. Not many Neanderthals lived in Europe at this time—maybe no more than twenty thousand in all of France—but they seemed to have adapted well to living along the edge of the glacier.

They apparently lived in close association. Two hundred living sites—all within twenty miles of one another—have been found in southern France. It is not certain, however, whether all the sites were inhabited at the same time. Most sites were under the overhangs of cliffs or in caves.

At one site stakes had been driven into the ground at the mouth of the cave. Skins were probably hung over them to keep out the

BRITAIN

BRITISH ICE SHEET

SCANDINAVIAN ICE SHEET

FRANCE

ALPINE ICE SHEET

ITALY

SPAIN

wind, rain, and snow. Heavy skin clothing must have been worn to combat the cold. The large teeth of Neanderthals suggest that they chewed hide to soften it, much as modern Eskimos do. The hearths were designed to give off heat as well as to cook food. Where wood was scarce, animal bones and fat were burned. Scientists have found underground pits or cellars that they think may have been used to store food during periods when the weather was too severe for hunting.

The Neanderthals were advanced culturally. Their lives were full of hazards, but they took care of their sick and old. They may have been the first to practice medicine. A number of Neanderthal fossils show signs of serious injuries that had completely healed long before death. Some of these individuals must have needed constant support and care. One had had an arm amputated and may have been blind. Neanderthals also were apparently familiar with medicinal plants. A man found in France had been buried on a bed of flowers sixty thousand years ago. All of the plants buried with him had medicinal qualities. Scientists think that he may have been a medicine man.

Ice-age Europe 70,000 to 35,000 years ago. Brown indicates Ice-Age coastline (British Isles joined to Europe) and the southern progress of ice sheets.

Neanderthal cave, like those found in southern
France, about 70,000 years ago

The Neanderthals were the first hominids known to have buried their dead. There is strong evidence that they conducted some kind of funeral ritual. Weapons, tools, and food, as well as flowers, were often placed in graves and the graves marked with animal horns or stones. Some caves were used as cemeteries. Twelve skeletons were found in one cave and a whole family in another.

There are also signs that Neanderthals practiced hunting rituals suggesting a primitive religion. Large stone vaults filled with ibex and cave bear skulls have been found. Recent discoveries of marked stones suggest that Neanderthals, and perhaps even earlier hominids, made and used symbolic images.

We don't know why these sensitive, progressive people became extinct. Some scientists suggest that as the glaciers receded, Cro-Magnons, a group of early *Homo sapiens sapiens,* invaded Europe and wiped them out. Others suggest that Neanderthals developed into modern humans. The most widely accepted theory is that the Neanderthals simply intermarried with the Cro-Magnons until they were absorbed by them. This theory is supported by the discovery of many caves in Israel containing remains that were a mixture of modern humans and Neanderthals. In any event, by thirty thousand years ago there were no more Neanderthals. *Homo sapiens sapiens* were the only type of *Homo* left on earth.

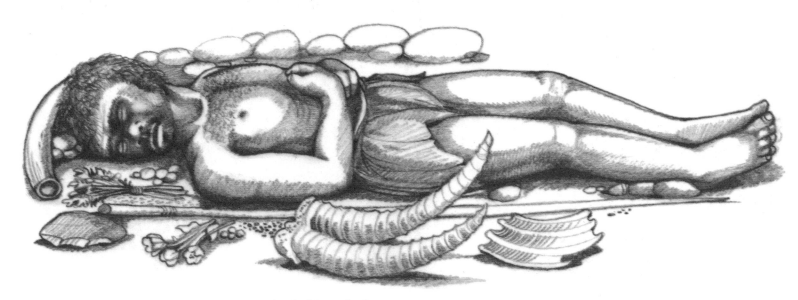

Neanderthal burial, showing tools, weapons, flowers, food

12.
HOMO SAPIENS SAPIENS
MODERN HUMANS

IT IS NOT KNOWN WHERE THE FIRST *HOMO SAPIENS SAPIENS* CAME from, or when they appeared. Some people suggest that they may have developed in many places at the same time; others say they first emerged in central Asia. However, most scientists believe that modern humans originated in Africa. The oldest known *Homo sapiens sapiens* fossils were discovered in African deposits that were fifty thousand years old.

There was an increase in population in Africa around fifty thousand years ago. Then, around forty thousand years ago—about the time of the beginning of the last Ice Age—severe droughts turned northern Africa into a desert. These events may have caused large groups of *Homo sapiens sapiens* to migrate into central Asia.

One of the earliest specimens of an early *Homo sapiens sapiens*, about 35,000 years old, from a Cro-Magnon site in France

101

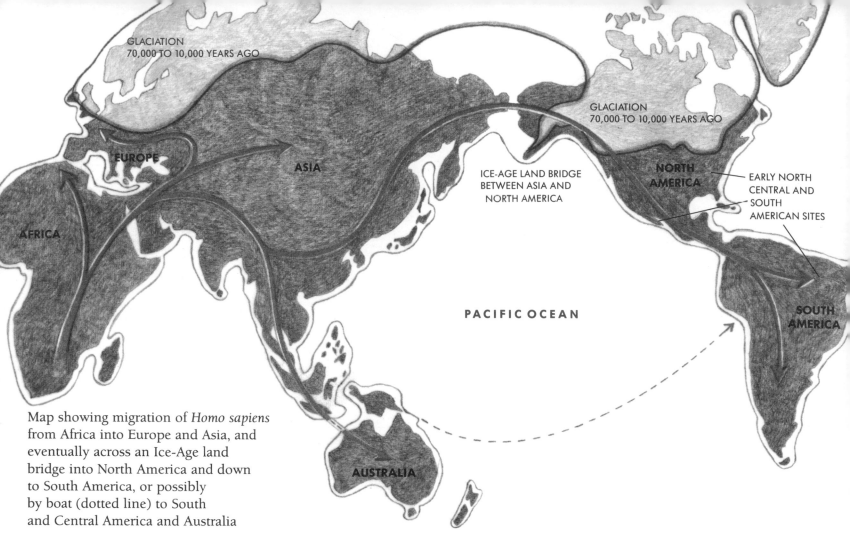

GLACIATION
70,000 TO 10,000 YEARS AGO

GLACIATION
70,000 TO 10,000 YEARS AGO

EUROPE

ASIA

AFRICA

ICE-AGE LAND BRIDGE
BETWEEN ASIA AND
NORTH AMERICA

NORTH
AMERICA

EARLY NORTH
CENTRAL AND
SOUTH
AMERICAN SITES

PACIFIC OCEAN

SOUTH
AMERICA

AUSTRALIA

Map showing migration of *Homo sapiens*
from Africa into Europe and Asia, and
eventually across an Ice-Age land
bridge into North America and down
to South America, or possibly
by boat (dotted line) to South
and Central America and Australia

Modern humans may have been wanderers by nature. By thirty
thousand years ago they had spread to almost every continent in
the world, including Australia and North and South America. There
is a great deal of controversy about when and where humans came
to the Americas. It was once thought that they migrated between
ten thousand and twenty thousand years ago. Several very old living sites discovered in South America suggest that they came much
earlier. The oldest of these, a rock shelter in Brazil known as Pedra
Furada, has been carbon-14 dated at thirty-two thousand years.
This rock shelter contained hearths, 560 stone tools, and cave art at
least as advanced as any of the same age found in Europe. Other
sites in South America, dated at thirteen thousand and fourteen
thousand years ago, and one in Mexico, dated at about twenty-four
thousand years ago, had equally advanced cultures. Such advanced
cultures suggest that humans had been in these areas considerably
earlier.

Some scientists now believe that humans may have crossed over to North America between forty thousand and thirty thousand years ago on a land bridge that connected Asia and North America. They suggest that humans then spread from North America into South America. The oldest known site in North America, however, is a rock shelter near Pittsburgh, Pennsylvania, called Meadowcroft, which has been dated at nineteen thousand years ago. This date is not accepted by everyone, however. Several sites in the western United States were originally thought to be somewhat older, but more reliable dating shows them to be no more than ten thousand years old. Many scientists are actively seeking the answer to this riddle.

Some scientists suggest that *Homo sapiens sapiens* may have arrived in the Americas by boat. Boats were almost certainly used to reach Australia. There was less water to cross then than there is now because much of the earth's water was frozen in the ice caps, resulting in lower water levels in the oceans.

In Europe, *H. sapiens sapiens* completely replaced the Neanderthals. For a long time it was thought that the more modern people had driven the Neanderthals out, but there is no evidence that this happened. In fact, the two groups apparently lived together peacefully for several thousand years. But the Neanderthals ultimately disappeared about thirty thousand years ago, and *H. sapiens sapiens* were the only hominids left on earth. Most scientists now think that as *H. sapiens sapiens* drifted slowly into Europe and Asia, they intermarried with the Neanderthals and gradually assimilated them.

The earliest known *H. sapiens sapiens* in Europe are called Cro-Magnons. The name means "big hole." They were named for the rock shelter in southwestern France where the first fossils—the remains of five individuals—were discovered. They were the oldest modern humans known at the time of their discovery. A wealth of other Cro-Magnon remains have since been recovered in Belgium, France, Germany, Gibraltar, Italy, and eastern and central Asia. Similar forms of modern humans have been found in Russia, China, Borneo, and all over Africa.

ICE SHEET

BRITAIN

GERMANY

FRANCE

Cro-Magnon   ICE SHEET

SPAIN

ITALY

ICE-AGE COASTLINE
70,000 TO 10,000 YEARS AGO

These groups varied greatly over time and space. Some of the earliest known modern humans were similar to the Neanderthals in some ways. They were short and their brains were about the same size but were shaped differently. Some had heavy brows, although not as pronounced as those of the Neanderthals. Almost all had thinner bones and longer arms and legs than Neanderthals. The bones of even the earliest known *Homo sapiens sapiens* were like those of modern humans in every respect. Their skulls, too, were shaped the same as those of modern humans. They had flattened faces with high, steep foreheads, protruding chins, and small front teeth. The structure of their brains seems to have been essentially the same as ours.

Cro-Magnon remains from Grotte des Enfants, France

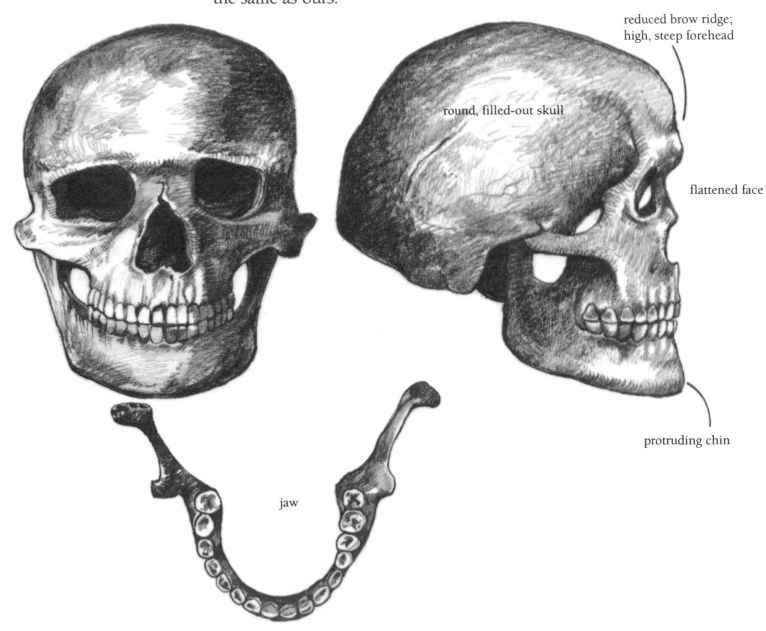

round, filled-out skull

reduced brow ridge; high, steep forehead

flattened face

protruding chin

jaw

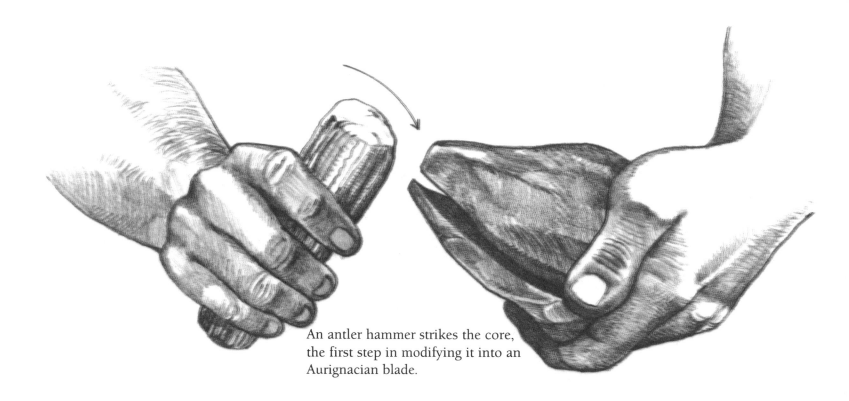

An antler hammer strikes the core, the first step in modifying it into an Aurignacian blade.

Although modern humans have changed little in appearance over forty thousand years, their culture has changed greatly. They have made more progress technologically and culturally in the last thirty thousand years than all of the other hominids put together in the previous three million years. Scientists think this may have been due to a better system of communication, perhaps language as we know it today.

The Cro-Magnons brought with them improved technology and a more sophisticated culture. Although they still made their living by hunting and gathering, their methods of food gathering were more efficient and their hunting techniques more effective than those of earlier groups. New types of animals were hunted, with emphasis on big game and herd animals.

The Cro-Magnon tool kit (which is known as the Aurignacian tool kit) was much better than that of the Neanderthals and included a greater variety of tools. Aurignacian blades were thinner and had sharper cutting edges and greater cutting and scraping surfaces. These blades could be made more quickly than those of the Neanderthals. Wooden or bone punches were used to strike the blades from the core stones.

Aurignacian blade

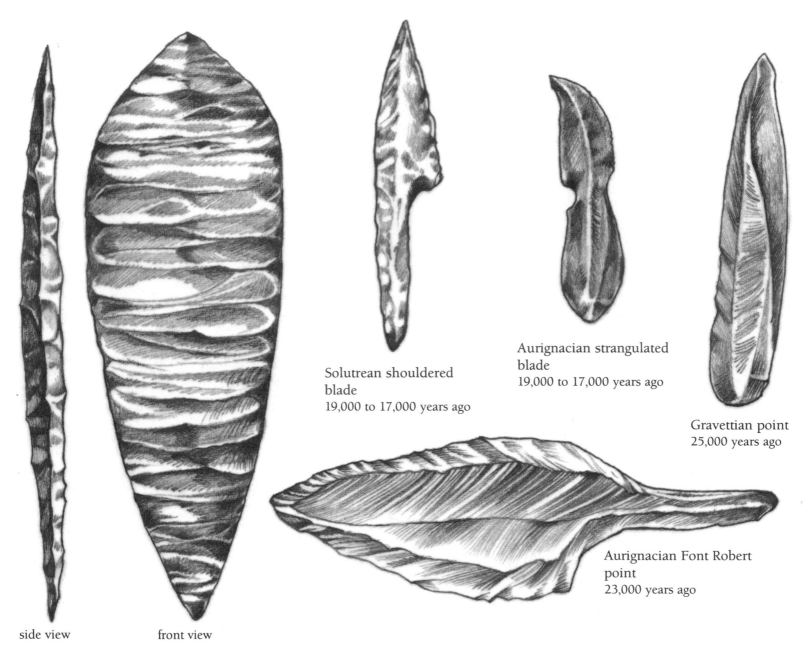

Solutrean shouldered blade
19,000 to 17,000 years ago

Aurignacian strangulated blade
19,000 to 17,000 years ago

Gravettian point
25,000 years ago

Aurignacian Font Robert point
23,000 years ago

side view   front view

Solutrean blade
20,000 years ago

Cro-Magnon Tool Kit

From the beginning, modern humans were more innovative and better able to adapt to local conditions than previous hominids. Unlike earlier hominids, who kept the same tool kit for tens of thousands and sometimes millions of years, *H. sapiens sapiens* developed many different cultures at the same time. Each culture evolved according to the particular requirements and food resources of a specific local area. The tool kit in one region was often quite different from that in a neighboring region, and the kits improved over time. The variety of tools increased and were better made. Sometimes these improvements took only a few thousand years to develop.

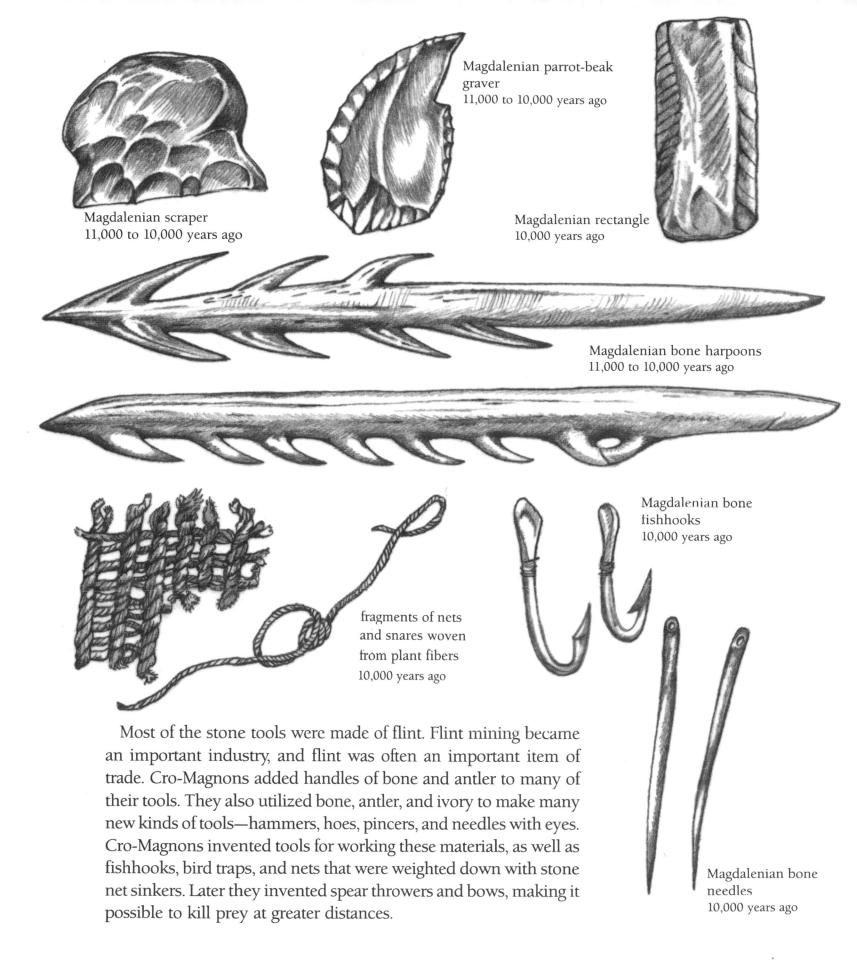

Magdalenian parrot-beak graver
11,000 to 10,000 years ago

Magdalenian scraper
11,000 to 10,000 years ago

Magdalenian rectangle
10,000 years ago

Magdalenian bone harpoons
11,000 to 10,000 years ago

Magdalenian bone fishhooks
10,000 years ago

fragments of nets and snares woven from plant fibers
10,000 years ago

Magdalenian bone needles
10,000 years ago

Most of the stone tools were made of flint. Flint mining became an important industry, and flint was often an important item of trade. Cro-Magnons added handles of bone and antler to many of their tools. They also utilized bone, antler, and ivory to make many new kinds of tools—hammers, hoes, pincers, and needles with eyes. Cro-Magnons invented tools for working these materials, as well as fishhooks, bird traps, and nets that were weighted down with stone net sinkers. Later they invented spear throwers and bows, making it possible to kill prey at greater distances.

Many Cro-Magnons were talented artists. They decorated tool handles with carvings showing the important events in their lives. Tiny animal figures were carved from mammoth ivory, bone, and antler, or molded from powdered bone mixed with clay. Their best-known artworks are the beautiful pictures that they painted on the walls of caves in France and Spain. Their invention of lamps, which burned animal fat, made this possible. At first the paintings were simple black outlines of animals and people. Later the outlines were filled in with colors made from powdered rocks mixed with animal fat. Similar paintings have been found in Africa. Many of these paintings can still be seen, although some are thirty thousand years old.

Some of the markings on tool handles may have been primitive calendars. Scientists believe that the Cro-Magnons were keeping track of seasonal changes as early as twenty-eight thousand years ago, long before writing was invented. These early humans may have marked time by the phases of the moon, much in the same manner that Native Americans did thousands of years later.

The pictures on cave walls also showed important events. Keeping track of when spring birds would arrive or salmon would come up the river or reindeer would migrate was important to the hunters' survival. Some of the images were abstract. Scientists think that writing and arithmetic developed from these abstractly pictured records. Such records may also have been an important factor in the first farming.

Woman carved from soapstone; Balzi Rossi, Italy, 20,000 years ago

Autumn bison and plant forms carved in a bone knife; from a cave at La Vache, Ice-Age France

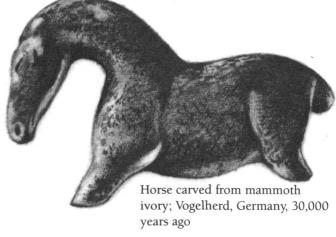

Horse carved from mammoth ivory; Vogelherd, Germany, 30,000 years ago

Female head carved from ivory; Brassempouy, France, 18,000 years ago

These new-type hominids decorated their clothing with shells and beads made of amber and polished ivory. Both men and women wore necklaces and bracelets made from animal teeth, shells, or beads carved from the ivory of mammoth tusks. Like tools, art objects in one region were sometimes quite different from those found in a neighboring region, and they changed over time.

The first modern humans were nomadic, following the game animals. They seem to have lived in large family groups. Some built tentlike structures inside cave entrances. Others lived in huts in forested areas. As better hunting methods developed, base camps were occupied for longer periods of time. Several families lived near one another. The number of people in a site varied with the type of game available.

By twenty thousand years ago more permanent homes were built. Long houses holding many families were made of stone blocks. There is evidence that communities of thirty to one hundred people lived together. Cooking pots and pottery were made from fired clay. Before this, pots were probably made of wood or leather. These excellent hunters roamed over wide areas and often came in contact with other groups with whom they traded.

Around fifteen thousand years ago huge herds of grass-eating animals roamed Europe, Asia, and North America. Groups of people began concentrating on hunting one particular kind of animal, such as mammoths or reindeer. People who moved into northern regions where there were no caves or trees built their houses from mammoth bones. They formed walls by placing skulls or leg bones in a circle and stacking other bones on top. Ribs or tusks were used for ceiling arches. These were covered with mammoth skins. Sometimes three or four houses were built close together and apparently occupied over many years.

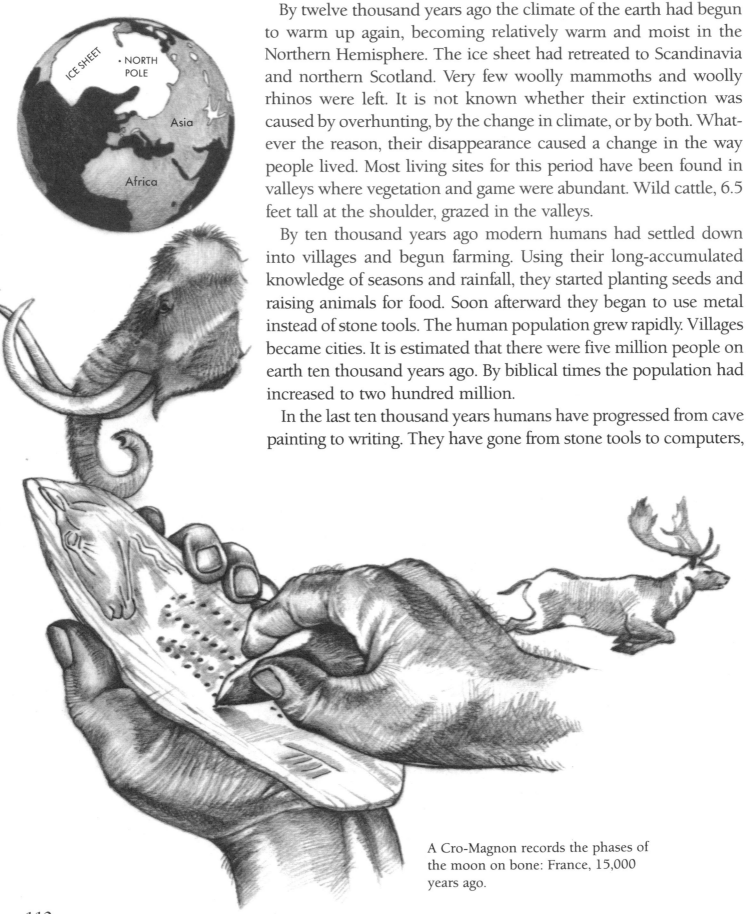

Polar view of earth during the last ice age showing extensive ice sheet (white) over Europe and Asia

ICE SHEET • NORTH POLE

Asia

Africa

By twelve thousand years ago the climate of the earth had begun to warm up again, becoming relatively warm and moist in the Northern Hemisphere. The ice sheet had retreated to Scandinavia and northern Scotland. Very few woolly mammoths and woolly rhinos were left. It is not known whether their extinction was caused by overhunting, by the change in climate, or by both. Whatever the reason, their disappearance caused a change in the way people lived. Most living sites for this period have been found in valleys where vegetation and game were abundant. Wild cattle, 6.5 feet tall at the shoulder, grazed in the valleys.

By ten thousand years ago modern humans had settled down into villages and begun farming. Using their long-accumulated knowledge of seasons and rainfall, they started planting seeds and raising animals for food. Soon afterward they began to use metal instead of stone tools. The human population grew rapidly. Villages became cities. It is estimated that there were five million people on earth ten thousand years ago. By biblical times the population had increased to two hundred million.

In the last ten thousand years humans have progressed from cave painting to writing. They have gone from stone tools to computers,

A Cro-Magnon records the phases of the moon on bone: France, 15,000 years ago.

112

from bows and arrows to hydrogen bombs, and from dugout canoes to the space shuttle. Four million years of accumulated knowledge made all this possible.

Scientists believe that people evolved because, from the beginning, it was necessary for hominids to work together to survive. Hominids were not swift runners like antelopes, large like mammoths, or fierce like wild boars. Very early they developed the cooperation and cleverness needed to get along with others in close social groups. Truly, hominids are relatives that modern humans can be proud of. Perhaps these traits, which are thought to have contributed to their survival, also made their brains grow. Certainly the traits of cooperative problem-solving are still very necessary for survival on earth. Modern humans must continue to evolve socially in order to meet the challenges of the future. Although all of the inventions made by modern humans show progress in mental ability, they do not always reflect progress in social relationships. Only by continuing to work together to find better ways of solving world problems can *Homo sapiens sapiens* hope to duplicate the million-year survival record set by their forebears.

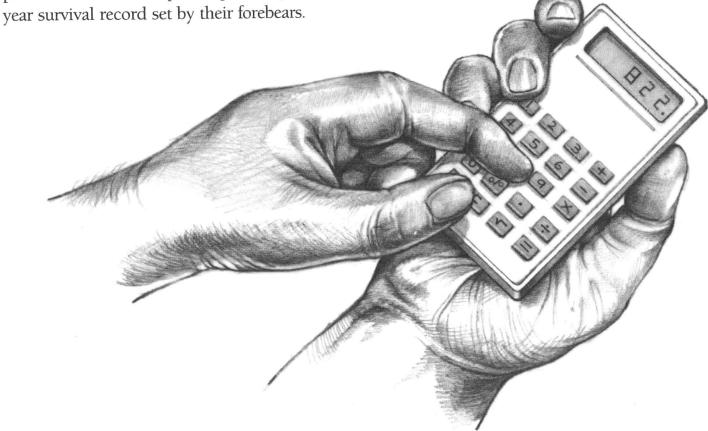

TIME CHART

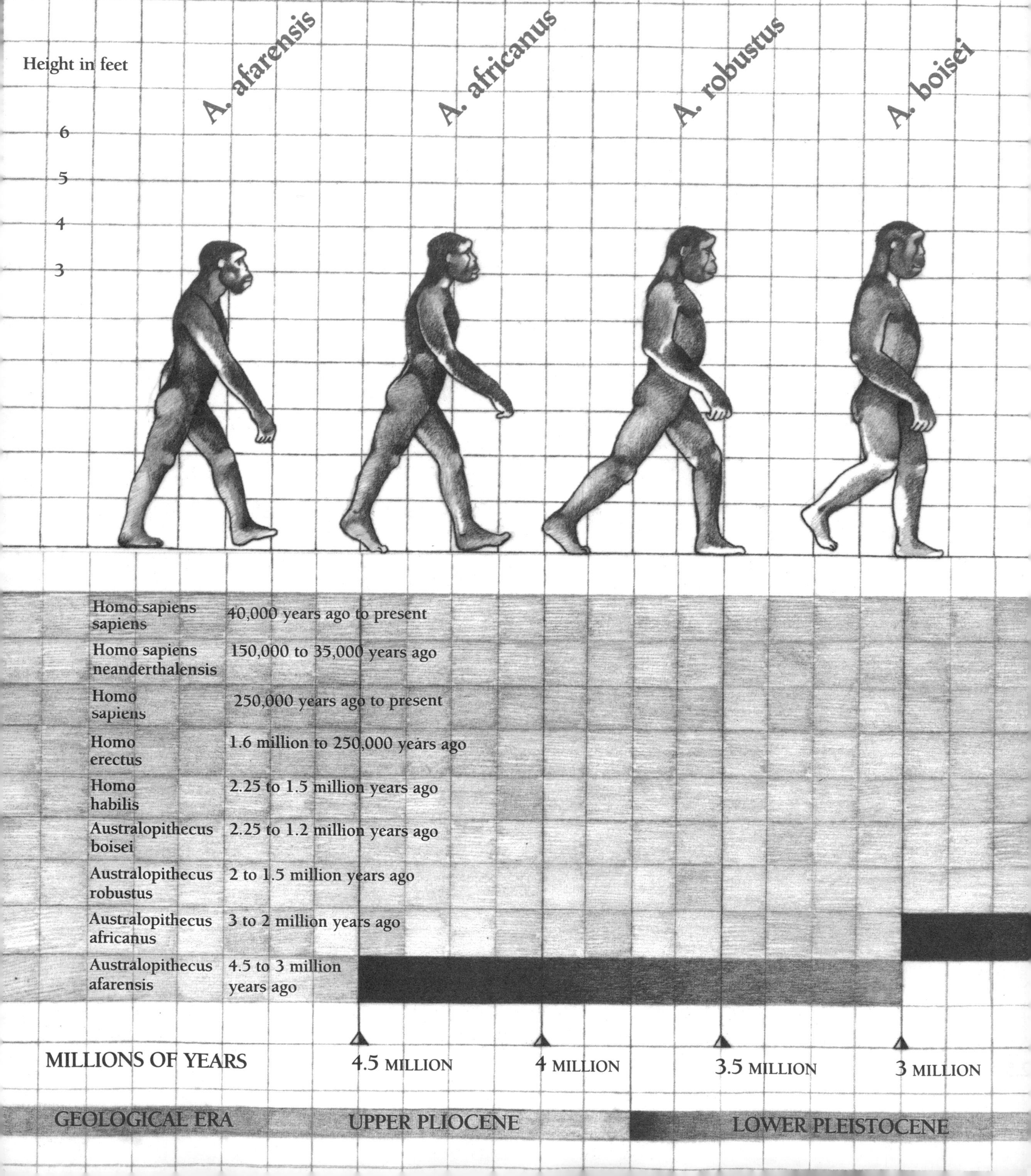

Height in feet

A. afarensis

A. africanus

A. robustus

A. boisei

6
5
4
3

Homo sapiens sapiens	40,000 years ago to present	
Homo sapiens neanderthalensis	150,000 to 35,000 years ago	
Homo sapiens	250,000 years ago to present	
Homo erectus	1.6 million to 250,000 years ago	
Homo habilis	2.25 to 1.5 million years ago	
Australopithecus boisei	2.25 to 1.2 million years ago	
Australopithecus robustus	2 to 1.5 million years ago	
Australopithecus africanus	3 to 2 million years ago	
Australopithecus afarensis	4.5 to 3 million years ago	

MILLIONS OF YEARS

4.5 MILLION   4 MILLION   3.5 MILLION   3 MILLION

GEOLOGICAL ERA   UPPER PLIOCENE   LOWER PLEISTOCENE

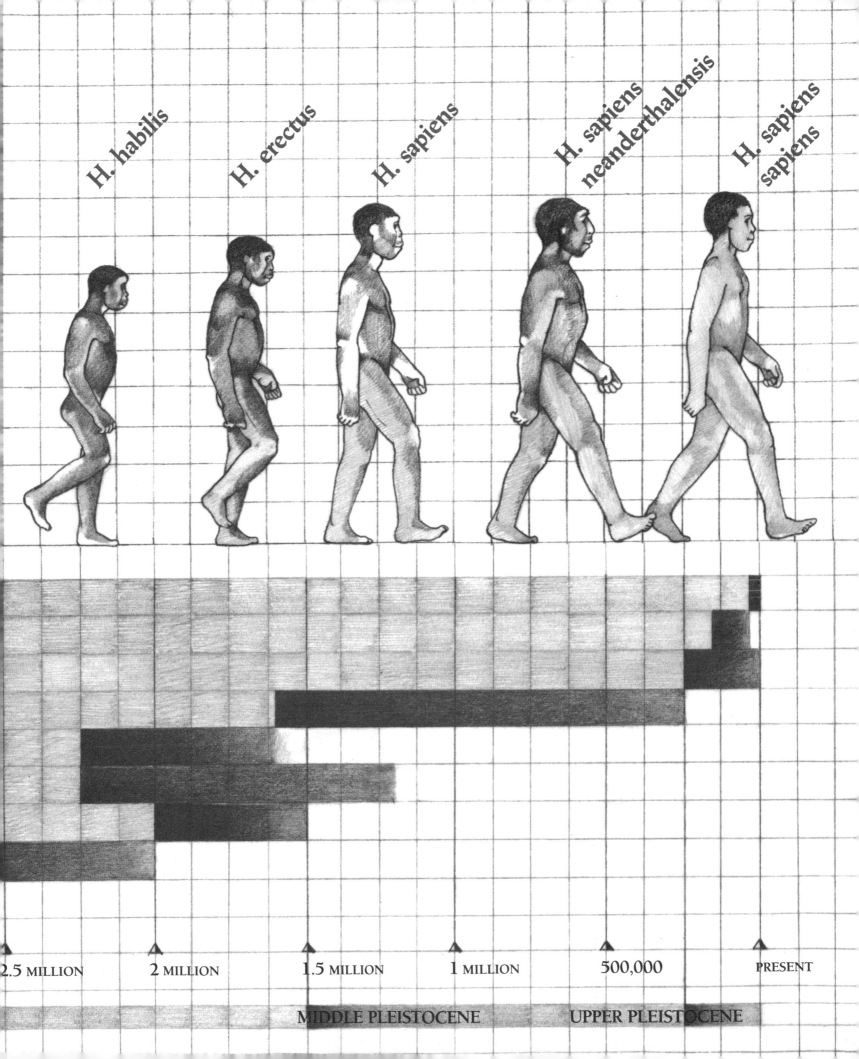

H. habilis

H. erectus

H. sapiens

H. sapiens
neanderthalensis

H. sapiens
sapiens

2.5 MILLION   2 MILLION   1.5 MILLION   1 MILLION   500,000   PRESENT

MIDDLE PLEISTOCENE   UPPER PLEISTOCENE

SPECIES CHART

Scientists group all living things into families. Families are divided into genera and species. The chart below shows the scientific names of the genera and species of Hominidae family.

Family: HOMINIDAE

Genus: *Australopithecus*
    Species: *Australopithecus afarensis*
        Australopithecus africanus
        Australopithecus robustus
        Australopithecus boisei

Genus: *Homo*
    Species: *Homo sapiens*
        Subspecies: archaic *Homo sapiens*
            Homo sapiens neanderthalensis
            Homo sapiens sapiens

BIBLIOGRAPHY

Adovasio, J. M., and Carlisle, R. C. "An Indian Hunters' Camp for 20,000 Years." *Scientific American,* May 1984, pp. 130–136.

Bray, Warwick. "Finding the Earliest Americans." *Nature,* June 29, 1986, p. 726.

Brain, C. K. *The Hunters or the Hunted?* Chicago: The University of Chicago Press, 1981.

————. "A Hominid Skull's Revealing Holes." *Natural History,* December 1974, pp. 44–45.

Ciochon, Russell L., and Corruccini, Robert S. *New Interpretations of Ape and Human Ancestry.* New York: Plenum Press, 1983.

Dillehay, Tom D. "A Late Ice-age Settlement in Southern Chile." *Scientific American,* October 1984, pp. 106–117.

Dobzhansky, Theodosius. *Mankind Evolving.* New Haven: Yale University Press, 1962.

Dolhinow, Phyllis, and Sarich, Vincent M. *Background for Man, Readings in Physical Anthropology.* Boston: Little, Brown and Company, 1971.

Gladkih, Mikhail I.; Kornietz, Ninelj L.; and Soffer, Olga. "Mammoth Bone Dwellings on the Russian Plain." *Scientific American,* November 1984, pp. 164–175.

Guiden, N., and Delibrias, G. "Carbon-14 Dates Point to Man in the Americas 32,000 Years Ago." *Nature,* June 19, 1986, pp. 769–771.

Hay, Richard L., and Leakey, Mary D. "The Fossil Footprints of Laetoli." *Scientific American,* February 1982, pp. 50–57.

Howells, William. *Mankind in the Making* (Revised edition). Garden City, New York: Doubleday & Company, 1967.

Johanson, Donald, and Edey, Maitland. "Lucy." *Science 81,* March 1981, pp. 44–55.

————. *Lucy, the Beginnings of Humankind.* New York: Warner Books, 1981.

Leakey, Louis S. B. "Adventures in the Search for Man." *National Geographic,* January 1963, pp. 132–152.

Leakey, Richard. *The Making of Mankind.* New York: E. P. Dutton, 1981.

Leakey, Richard, and Walker, Alan. "*Homo erectus* Unearthed/A Fossil Skeleton 1,600,000 Years Old." *National Geographic,* November 1985, pp. 624–629.

Lewin, Roger. "New Fossil Upsets Human Family." *Science,* August 15, 1986, pp. 720–721.

————. "Unexpected Anatomy in *Homo erectus.*" *Science,* November 2, 1984, p. 529.

McCord, Anne. *The Children's Picture Prehistory of Early Man.* London: Usborne Publishing Ltd., 1977.

O'Brien, Eileen M. "What Was the Acheulean Hand Ax?" *Natural History,* July 1984, pp. 20–24.

Pfeiffer, John E. *The Emergence of Man.* New York: Harper & Row, 1978.

————. "Current Research Casts New Light on Human Origins." *Smithsonian,* June 1980, pp. 91–103.

Pilbeam, David. "The Descent of Hominoids and Hominids." *Scientific American,* March 1984, pp. 84–96.

Poirier, Frank E. *In Search of Ourselves.* Minneapolis: Burgess Publishing Company, 1974

Potts, Richard, and Shipman, Pat. "Cutmarks Made by Stone Tools on Bones from Olduvai Gorge, Tanzania." *Nature,* June 18, 1981, pp. 577–580.

Reader, John. *Missing Links, The Hunt for Earliest Man.* Boston: Little, Brown and Company, 1981.

Reichs, Kathleen J. *Hominid Origins: Inquiries Past and Present.* Washington, D.C.: University Press of America, 1983.

Rensberger, Boyce. "Bones of Our Ancestors." *Science 84,* April 1984, pp. 29–39.

Rukang, Wu, and Shenglong, Lin. "Peking Man." *Scientific American,* June 1983, pp. 86–94.

Shipman, Pat. "Baffling Limb on the Family Tree." *Discover,* September 1986, pp. 87–93.

Smith, Fred H., and Spencer, Frank. *The Origins of Modern Humans.* New York: Alan R. Liss, 1984.

Stringer, Christopher B. "Fate of the Neanderthal." *Natural History,* December 1984, pp. 6–12.

Tattersall, Ian, and Delson, Eric. *Ancestors/Four Million Years of Humanity.* New York: American Museum of Natural History, 1984.

Walker, A.; Leakey, R. E.; Harris, J. M.; and Brown, F. H. "2.5-Myr *Australopithecus boisei* from West of Lake Turkana, Kenya." *Nature,* August 7, 1986, pp. 517–522.

Washburn, S. L., and Moore, Ruth. *Ape Into Human.* Boston: Little, Brown and Company, 1980.

Weaver, Kenneth F. "Stones, Bones, and Early Man/The Search for Our Ancestors." *National Geographic,* November 1985, pp. 561–623.

White, Tim. "Evolutionary Implications of Pliocene Hominid Footprints." *Science,* April 11, 1980, pp. 175–176.

Wood, B. A. *Human Evolution.* New York: John Wiley & Sons, 1978.

INDEX

HELEN RONEY SATTLER

remembers growing up with "a reverence for books, a thirst for knowledge," and a firm belief that "there wasn't a thing I couldn't do if I set my mind to it." She was born in Iowa, grew up on a farm in Missouri, and graduated cum laude from Southwest Missouri State College with a Bachelor of Science degree in education. She taught elementary school for nine years and was a children's librarian for one year.

Ms. Sattler began writing stories for her son when he was small and later wrote several stories that she sold to magazines. Two of her early books for Lothrop, *Train Whistles* and *Recipes for Art and Craft Materials,* have been reissued in updated editions. Her grandson's fascination with dinosaurs, and the inadequate materials available for young readers, suggested a direction for her work that has established her as a leading science writer for children. Her award-winning books include *Dinosaurs of North America* and *The Illustrated Dinosaur Dictionary. Pterosaurs, the Flying Reptiles; Baby Dinosaurs; Sharks, the Super Fish;* and *Whales, the Nomads of the Sea,* like their predecessors, have been warmly praised by reviewers.

Ms. Sattler has traveled widely to do research for her books. She lives with her husband in Bartlesville, Oklahoma.

CHRISTOPHER SANTORO

was born and raised in Connecticut and received a Bachelor of Fine Arts degree from the Rhode Island School of Design. Following graduation he moved to New York City and began working as a designer and illustrator. His artwork has been exhibited in shows, and he has illustrated more than twenty highly praised children's books of all kinds, including *Pterosaurs, the Flying Reptiles* by Helen Roney Sattler. He especially likes drawing pictures of prehistoric subjects because his "childhood interest in things like dinosaurs never faded." Mr. Santoro recently moved from Manhattan to New Hampshire, where he is building a new home.